THE WOLF BLOGS

The Wolf Blogs

Surviving My Covert Narcissist Husband

An Unfiltered Story of Narcissistic Trauma

JENNIFER IOLITE

LNAL LIFE LLC

Copyright © 2024 by LNAL Life LLC
Atlanta, Georgia

No part of this publication may be reproduced, stored in a retrieval system, or transmitted in any form or by any means, electronic, mechanical, photocopying, recording, scanning, or otherwise, except as permitted under Sections 107 or 108 of the 1976 United States Copyright Act, without the prior written permission of the Publisher. Requests to the Publisher for permission should be addressed to the Permissions Department, LNAL Life LLC, 691 John Wesley Dobbs Avenue, NE, Suite V150, Atlanta, GA 30312.

Limit of Liability/Disclaimer of Warranty: The Publisher and the author make no representations or warranties with respect to the accuracy or completeness of the contents of this work and specifically disclaim all warranties, including without limitation warranties of fitness for a particular purpose. No warranty may be created or extended by sales or promotional materials. The advice and strategies contained herein may not be suitable for every situation. This work is sold with the understanding that the Publisher is not engaged in rendering medical, legal, or other professional advice or services. If professional assistance is required, the services of a competent professional person should be sought. Neither the Publisher nor the author "liable for damages arising herefrom. The fact that an individual, organization, or website is referred to in the work as a citation and/or potential source of further information does not mean that the author or the Publisher endorses the information the individual, organization, or website may provide or recommendations they/it may make. Further, readers should be aware that websites listed in this work may have changed or disappeared between when this work was written and when it is read.

LNAL Life LLC publishes its books in a variety of electronic and print formations. Some content that appears in print may not be available in the electronic books, and vice versa.

TRADEMARKS: LNAL Life LLC logo are trademarks in the United States and other countries and may not be used without written permission. All other trademarks are the property of their respective owners. LNAL Life LLC is not associated with any product or vendor mentioned in this book.

Interior and Cover Design:
Danna Mathias of Dearly Creative LLC

Paperback ISBN: 978-1-7376637-8-2
eBook ISBN: 978-1-7376637-9-9

CONTENTS

Chapter 1: The Therapist's Suggestion	1
Chapter 2: Seeking Solace in Old Movies	14
Chapter 3: Shrinking into Oblivion	35
Chapter 4: The Ultimate Betrayal	53
Chapter 5: The Numbness of Survival	72
Chapter 6: The Breaking Point	79
Chapter 7: The Line in the Sand	96
Chapter 8: The Numbness of Despair	115
Chapter 9: The Futile Coping Mechanisms	135
Chapter 10: The Glimmer of Hope	150
Chapter 11: The Struggle of Acceptance	158
Chapter 12: The Non-Linear Path of Healing	170
Chapter 13: The Unraveling	178
Chapter 14: The Breaking Point and the Beginning of Healing	188
Epilogue: A Survivor's Reflection	195
Resources To Thrive After Narcissistic Abuse	199

INTRODUCTION

Content Warning: This book contains coarse language, references to polyamory and discussions of suicide. Some content may be emotionally challenging for certain readers. Please read with discretion.

This book is a chronicle of the last year of my emotionally abusive marriage. It's important to note that this is a raw and unfiltered account of a woman in an abusive marriage with a man insisting that she agree to his demands of polyamorous relationships. If you understand anything about polyamory, you know that consent with all parties is of primary importance. I never consented but was manipulated, bullied and shamed into agreeing to his conditions. If you've been in a similar situation, or close to one, reading this may be distressing.

I started this blog at the suggestion of our marriage therapist. I was scared to be too forthcoming initially, fearing the potential consequences when my husband read it. I should have known better. He couldn't have been bothered to care about what I felt or how miserable I was at the time.

I already suffered through all the forms of narcissistic abuse for over a decade: gaslighting, silent treatment, projection, stone walling, word salad, and more. Honestly, I'm lucky to be alive, but I'm getting ahead of myself.

It's been six years since I last looked at this blog. As I read it again after so long, I'm struck by the pain and suffering that leap off the pages. The very real and tormenting agony of the woman writing it - the woman that was me - is hardly recognizable now.

Yes, I recall the incidents and how they tore at my heart and my mind, but the woman I was then is most definitely not the woman I am now.

When I consider the final post (disregarding the post-script entry), written just before I began to truly understand what had been happening, I'm greatly saddened by the depth of despair in the words. At the same time, I'm immensely relieved that I managed to survive another day.

This book is broken up by month. Each month begins with a short description of the current state of the situation, followed by the unaltered blog posts I wrote in my desperate moments; trying to understand what was happening to me.

At the end of the book, you'll find a list of resources that helped me, and some that continue to help me, recover from the very real trauma of emotional abuse. If you find yourself in a similar situation, please get the help you need. I send you my most heartfelt love and encouragement.

This is my story, a journey through narcissistic trauma, and a testament to the resilience of the human spirit. If you see yourself in these pages, know that you are not alone, and that there is hope for healing and transformation.

CHAPTER 1
The Therapist's Suggestion

OCTOBER

Going to a therapist had been my idea. After just one year of marriage, my husband decided that he was polyamorous. At the time, I didn't know much about it, so I did some reading. The truth was, he wanted permission to cheat although I didn't understand that at the time. I indicated that I wasn't interested in that type of relationship with him. It wasn't that I was a prude; it was just that it wasn't how I was wired. Nor how I wanted to live.

Despite my hesitation and discomfort, my husband told me that that was the way it was going to be. Given that we had a pseudo Master/submissive relationship (mostly in the bedroom, or so I thought), I sucked it up and tried to support him. I just made myself miserable in the process.

After going to marriage counseling for several years and finding myself still slipping into deeper depression and misery, our therapist suggested an outlet for my emotions: a blog. By this point, the therapist had really become mine since my husband kept telling me that I was the one with the problem. He rarely attended sessions.

As I read back through these posts, it's interesting to see myself recognizing that it was my choice to stay when I didn't feel like I had a choice at all. He had insisted I quit my VP position a year earlier, leaving me financially dependent on someone for the first time in my life.

I also find it intriguing that my focus at the time was on his behavior as someone insisting on being polyamorous rather than the obvious manipulation that was going on. It's clear to me now that his desire for an open relationship was just another way to control and emotionally abuse me.

In this chapter, you'll read the raw and unfiltered posts from the early days of my blog, as I struggled to make sense of my husband's actions and my own feelings. It's a glimpse into the confusion, pain, and desperation that consumed me during this dark period of my life.

11th – Misery in Mono/Poly Land

More years than I care to recall ago, my Master started the slow misery of my world by announcing that he was Poly. He told me that he had always felt that way but society made him feel it was bad and so he didn't acknowledge it as a possible way to live.

I felt like my world had been turned upside down. The bliss and adoration of my husband and Master was shattered. I felt angry, betrayed, extreme sadness and all the other things that you might expect.

I want to support my husband and Master in his choice. Since I'm anything but a prude (I enjoy being submissive in the bedroom), I decided I should learn as much as I can about this form of lifestyle. I read and read and read. Books and blogs and websites. I go to poly meetups, support groups, couple and personal counseling.

- I'm angry when I read poly elitists state that I'm old-fashioned (I most certainly am not). Or just state that I'm flat out wrong for feeling this way. Well, guess what, fuck you and your holier-than-thou poly shit. That isn't a real way to convince me; by shaming and discounting my feelings.
- I'm shocked when someone tells me that I should get a divorce because we are doomed.
- I'm sad when I try to figure out my boundaries, only to be told that even the small step I try to make is not possible.
- I'm hurt when I feel like my Master gets to have fun while I'm stuck at home with our child.

- I'm hopeless when I feel stuck in a situation that makes me unhappy.

Generally, I'm just miserable. I've been taking anti-anxiety meds for 6 months and am still on the verge of sobbing all the time. Whenever my Master goes on a date, I take more meds and try to smile at my daughter. When he tells me that he loves me, I think I feel it but I'm still overwhelming sad.

I don't even know why I'm writing anything down. I guess because I feel so isolated and alone. It's not a fun place to be.

This is not who I am.
I am not a miserable person.
But I guess I am.

12th – The Edge

I live on the edge but not in a good way.

The edge of:

- tears
- nausea
- nothingness
- sobbing uncontrollably
- laying down and not getting up
- running away

14th – Numb and Joyless

It doesn't please me to tell you that I'm numb right now.

The anti-anxiety meds keep me from breaking down into a puddle of tears but also rob me of my personality. I'll also admit that I'm drinking more than I usually do. Something I'm not proud of. I'm not getting drunk per se, just having more than I usually do (3 or 4 glasses of wine instead of 2, 3 cocktails instead of 1 or 2).

The things I usually find joyful with leave me feeling, well, meh.

- I love growing my business and meeting new people to interact with but I know that I'm not coming across with the genuine enthusiasm that I used to have.
- I love to make music with my friends in a band but I've not attended a rehearsal in a month because I just can't face them. I can't face having to be 'happy' when I feel anything but happy.
- I love to knit and create new patterns and I haven't picked up the needles in months.
- I love cooking and trying new recipes. Ho hum.
- I love smelling the wind and the scent of the season (whatever it might be). I don't even notice it now.

I've lost my bliss and my joy.

I want it back.

26th – Choose Your Hard

I read so much.

I read about all the different perspectives about poly relationships.
- Mono/poly
- Poly/poly
- Poly/mono
- How to try harder to make it work
- How poly is an orientation similar to the LGBT community.

Oh, that's the one. That's the one that get my fur up.
Really!?! An orientation?
I call BS.
It doesn't feel like it to me.
Poly is a choice.
A conscious choice.

I can try harder.
I can read more. And more.
I can try to understand how he can love me and still want to be with other women.
I can try to understand how he can love me while I'm sobbing at his choice.
I can try to be happy that he is happy while I'm miserable.
I can take medication to make me numb and not care that my husband and Master dates and fucks many other women.
I can smile and defend his choice to our daughter (while attempting to teach her to be tolerant).
I can pretend that I don't care that he comes home smelling like some other woman.

I can get up each morning and get through my day (and it feels like sleepwalking).
But I'm dying inside.
A soul-crushing death.

But of course, the polys would say I'm not trying hard enough.
So I guess I'll try harder.

29th – Darkness

There is only darkness now.
But not black enough for me.

Where is there a hole deep enough and dark enough for me to hide?
The sun shines brightly today but not enough to brighten my heart.
My soul is full of darkness.
My body is numb.
There is nothing.
Nothing to fill me with happiness.
Joy has left the building of my life.

I only want to crawl in the dark hole and stay there.
Let the blackness surround the blackness inside me.

There is no hand that can reach me to pull me out of the darkness.
Nothing to show me that the flowers can bloom again.
Flowers I buy for myself to show the beauty of living, only fade and die.
The same way I that I have died inside.
No beauty.
Only misery.
Only despair.
No joy.
No meaning.
Hopelessness.
Mourning for what is lost.
Mourning for the love that filled me full of bliss.
Mourning for adventures had with my love.
Gone forever.

Nothing to look forward to except more darkness.
Waiting for it to engulf me completely.
So I don't see or feel the darkness anymore.

30th – Alone

Polyamory doesn't work.
It doesn't work.

Maybe for some but not for me.
It leaves me feeling empty.
Alone.

Alone when my Master goes on a date to fuck many other women.
Alone when my Master falls asleep instead of coming home.
Alone when my Master finally comes home.
Alone when my Master touches me.
Alone when my Master kisses me.
Alone when my Master smells like some other woman.
Alone when my Master fucks me.
Alone when my Master holds me close.
Alone when my Master whispers his love to me.

I am alone and dead inside.

30th – Choice and the Runaway

This deep and dreadful feeling of despair is ceaseless.
I don't want it anymore.
Sure, you can say it is my choice.
In fact, I say it to myself.

My choice.
Certainly, it is my choice to stay when I am consumed by anguish.
So, do I stay and continue to feel so wholly despondent?
I am empty.
Nothing to give.
Nothing to do except go through the motions of my life.

The life I adored so completely until...
Until I was poly-bombed (while I despise that word, it suits).
Until the rug of my perfect life was whisked away from beneath me.
Until everything I cherished became unbearable.

My choice.

To stay:
Continue to be hopelessness and empty.
Until my Master tires of the barren and lifeless body that is my own.
And his.
Tires of the emptiness that is inside me.
Until my Master despises and resents me.

To go:
Where to go?
Someplace else.
Someplace far away.
Someplace to hide.
Someplace to be until the darkness takes the pain away.

I don't know if I have the strength left to decide.

CHAPTER 2
Seeking Solace in Old Movies

NOVEMBER

I found myself trying to justify my husband's actions through movies such as The Women. I was heartbroken and unhappy, seeking solace anyplace I could. Old movies were one way I tried to make sense of it all.

Looking back, it is so obvious that I was broken. My spirit was shattered, and I felt like it was beyond repair.

I was cold and alone, dealing with a situation I desperately wanted out of. I felt trapped, with no clear way to escape the emotional turmoil that had become my daily life.

During this time, I even questioned my own sexual identity and found myself wanting. Wanting to not have a label placed on me, at least not one that I didn't define myself.

The truth is, I am a monogamist. There's nothing to be ashamed of; it's just how I'm wired.

Do others have to live the same way I do? Of course not. But as I read many times, a polyamorous relationship should only go as fast as the slowest person. I guess that's true for a lot of things in life. Being forced or manipulated into going faster always ends with someone getting hurt.

That someone was me.

As you read this chapter, you'll witness the depths of my despair as I struggled to come to terms with my own needs and desires while being pressured to accept a lifestyle that went against everything I believed in. You'll see me grasping at straws, trying to find some way to justify the unjustifiable, all while my sense of self slowly crumbled away.

It's a painful journey, but one that ultimately led me to a greater understanding of who I am and what I deserve in a relationship.

6th - Keep Still

I'm a fan of classic movies. Gone With The Wind, The Thin Man, Bell Book and Candle, Ball of Fire, and, The Women. The Women from 1939 (don't waste your time on the 2008 version). For those not familiar with the movie, is based on a Broadway play that features, you guessed it, only women. The plot focuses on Mary Haynes and her cheating husband and her busybody friends. There are an amazing number of one-liners delivered by some incredible actresses: Marjorie Main (better known as MaKettle), Paulette Goddard (known best for her role in Kitty), RosalindRussell (better known as Auntie Mame but my favorite is His Girl Friday) among others.

However, my favorite character is the lead: Norma Shearer. She was an amazing woman in so many ways. The role as Mary Haines feels so true to her. Historians called her "the exemplar of sophisticated 1930s womanhood...exploring love and sex with an honesty that would be considered frank by modern standards". Shearer is celebrated as a feminist pioneer, "the first American film actress to make it chic and acceptable to be single and not a virgin on screen". This almost revolutionary spirit appeals to me. I feel like have the ability to be strong, vibrant and then turn all that on its head to be a submissive to my husband.

I've seen this movie many many times but I've watched it a lot lately. It doesn't seem to matter that it is from almost 80 years ago, the message is clear to me. If you love your husband (or partner), you need to keep your mouth shut if they cheat. This holds true for me in a mono/poly relationship too. My Master isn't cheating (according to him). He is open and transparent and so very loving (to a point). I'm sure many would say that I am living a lie. I don't think it is that black and white.

Mary's mother tells her early in the movie, 'Keep still, my baby. Keep still even though you ache to speak.' This one sentence is the key for me.

Keep still.
Keep still even though my heart breaks.
Keep still even while I choke down the sobs.
Keep still and smile.
Keep still and try to find my way.
Keep still and collaborate joyfully with my husband.
Keep still to have peace and joy again.
Keep still and reach for the light.
I know I will reach it.
I just want it soon.

11th – Frozen

My heart is frozen.
The barren winterscape of my love is cold.
I am cold.
Cold inside.

So cold that it hurts to breathe.
So I stop.
Breathing.

To breathe means hurt.
Pain.
To breathe means to cry.
Frozen tears fall upon my warm face.

Frozen because I must protect my heart.
From being hurt.
Hurt so wholly.
A heart frozen to keep the blood from pouring out.
Pouring out my anguish.

Frozen to contain the torment.
Frozen to the world.
Frozen to my Master.
Frozen to myself.

No warmth or love to share from my frozen heart.

15th – Alternate Universe

Tonight, as I'm quietly reading at home I get a text
It's from one of them
One of the ones that *says* she is my friend
The one that introduced him to poly
The one that chases him shamelessly
The truth is, she just wants to be at my house
Drinking my booze
Getting drunk
And hoping to see my husband
I'm NOT that dumb (or perhaps I am since I let her come over)

Anyway, she asks to come over
I reply that he is traveling
She insists
Sigh
Ok

After getting a big drink
She plops down on the floor in the den
I can tell she is upset
Agitated
Eyes red
Oh dear
What boy incident now?
I prepare to be sympathetic

Then, tearfully, she tells me
My husband has dumped her
She sobs
I gape

I have no words
She is crying to ME about MY husband dumping her
When I've asked her repeatedly to stop chasing him
(Her reply was that it was up to him to tell her and fuck you very much Jennifer)

After staring at her for what fells like hours
I find some words
I make excuses for him
I say he is working a lot
I say he is traveling a lot
I say he is needing more time for himself
I can't believe it is coming out of my mouth
Never in a million years would I have thought
I would be making excuses for my s-o-b husband to one of his side pieces

I must be in an alternate universe

19th - Happy

Many in the poly world, the poly elitists, say that to be a good partner, you must be happy for your partner to have another.

If you are a rational person, a thinking person, a person not stuck in old-fashioned views, you must be happy for your partner to get busy with another person.

They call it compersion.

The made up word by the polys for the so-called joyful feeling that you have when your spouse had a great time banging someone else.

There is no such word.
Go ahead, look it up, I'll wait.

It doesn't exist in the dictionary.
The polys made it up to make themselves feel better about fucking other people while their spouse is at home miserable.

Sure, I want my husband to be happy.
I like it when he is happy.
I'm delighted when he feels his power.
I'm even more delighted when he feels his power over me.

When he comes home after being with some other woman (not the word I want to use but I'll be polite), I can't say I feel like doing the happy dance for him.
In fact, I don't even want him to touch me.
I'm about as far from happy as I can be.

I guess I'm not rational.
Or a thinking person.
I must be old-fashioned (although no one I know would say I was that in any way, shape or form).

I'm not happy.
Despite trying to be.
I'm miserable.

Happiness doesn't live here anymore.

20th – Broken

Sometimes I feel broken.
Broken by my husband's desire to fuck other women.
Broken by my despair and hopelessness.
Broken by the loss of a love that was blissful.

I'm not actually broken.
It's not me that is broken.
It is my relationship with my Master and husband.

The relationship is broken.
The connection between us is broken.

The connection that was so dear to us both.
This connection is damaged.
I try to act like nothing is wrong.
When I do, my actions feel insincere.
I know he feels the loss as well.
A loss that is tempered by his NRE (New Relationship Energy: another stupid phrase the polys have invented).
He doesn't feel the broken I feel.
He only feels the arms, lips, vagina and ass of some other woman.
It dulls his broken.
Like some kind of medicine.
I guess I'm glad he is spared some of the agony.

It is sharp and painful to me as walking on broken glass.
A knife shoved into my chest each time he mentions one of his many metamours (another one of those made up poly words).
I feel every moment of pain.
Flinch at the smell of some other woman on his lips.

The knowing that he was fucking her just hours before coming home to conquer me.

My reaction?
I shut down.
I can't stand the pain.
I want it to stop.
I want to jump off the glass and find a way to soothe my tortured heart.

Can we repair the broken?
Can the connection be mended?

I don't know.
I know of no glue to fix it.
No amount of talking seems to fix it.
No amount of affection eases the sorrow.
As long as my Master continues on this path, our home and love is broken.

22nd – From Radical Monogamy to Polyamory (and all the stuff in between)

I was recently referred to as a radical monogamist.
I wasn't familiar with the terms so I asked what was meant.
This person said that I was fully and passionately in love with my husband and he was the most exciting thing for me.
True.
But that I also was not opposed to having relationships/sex with others because my Master is the one that truly excites me.
Also true.
Anyone other than my Master was just 'condiments' to my sex life.
All this made sense to me.

However, I wanted to know more about this concept and hence, did research.
What I found was NOT the definition presented to me.

Most of what I found about radical monogamy states:
The Christian teaching about marriage is radical, unconditional monogamy.
OR
Radical monogamy being the rejection of even serial monogamy.

In between, is what is called serial monogamy.
The practice of engaging in a succession of monogamous sexual relationships.

Another in between, would be swinging:
A non-monogamous behavior in which both singles and partners in a committed relationship engage in sexual activities with others as a recreational or social activity.

And finally, we end up with polyamory:

The practice of, or desire for, intimate relationships where individuals may have more than one partner, with the knowledge and consent of all partners. It has been described as "consensual, ethical and responsible non-monogamy".

One of the interesting things I read is that the polyamory community, by and large, refuses any definition that describes how poly works. In one sense, that is quite liberating and in another, quite frustrating when you are trying to navigate through your own experience.

The poly community likes to say they are open an welcoming to everyone. EXCEPT swingers. Many blogs and posts I find state things like:

Swingers tend of focus on compartmentalizing sex and feelings; they often believe that it is not possible to have feelings of attachment to more than one person at the same time.

It is sad really, that those that tell others to be tolerant of their choice of lifestyle are so militantly anti-swinger. What makes you so much better than others that practice their own form of consensual non-monogamy?

I find that my husband is the one person that I have opened every bit of me to have and hold. I find that depth of connection the most exciting thing I have ever experienced.

Do I want other men (or women)? Maybe. I'm less excited about the people and more excited about how I could be with other men and have it please my Master. Do I want to have a relationship with these people? Sure, I want to at least like this person since my largest erogenous zone is between my ears and connecting on some level is the first step towards any relationship, sexual or otherwise.

I find that it is not so black and white.

And who are the polys trying to kid? I mean, if you love someone and it is nonsexual, then you are close friends (I have several male and female friends like this). So, if you are calling yourself poly, when you intend to have sex with another person. Your level of like or love can vary greatly.

Who gave the poly community exclusivity to caring and friendship?

I found this essay good when it stated:
Polyamorists have an idea in their head of what "swinging" is, and it's not actually what most swinging is (although sometimes it is). Many swingers are mutual friends. Or become such. Or are looking for such. Or prefer such. And friendship is love. And wanting friendship is wanting love. And that's poly.

I guess you could say I've been a serial monogamist most of my life. Married, divorced, serious, exclusive relationships and finally followed by marriage.

However, I'm NOT excited about my Master going off to fuck some other women without me just to come home and want to tell me about it while smelling like her.

It doesn't excite me.
It freezes me.
It shuts any passion I have for him.
I shut the door of my heart on him.
No longer does he have access to my deepest emotions.

No longer do we have the depth of connection that we did.

So no, I guess I'm not a radical monogamist nor a polyamorist. I'm something in the middle.
I find the middle of the road is a hard place to walk.

23rd – Mourning

Black is the traditional attire of a mourning spouse.
Those most affected by the loss of a loved one often observe a period of grieving.
This can be marked by withdrawal from social events and quiet, respectful behavior.

I am in mourning.
I have lost my love.
I have lost the thing that made me thrill each day.
I have lost the connection with my husband that filled me with overwhelming bliss.

I can no longer have sex with my husband.
It is too painful.
Painful to know that he goes out to fuck other women.
Try as I might, I cannot open myself to him.
The connection we had when we made love is gone.
It is no longer love-making.
It is just plain ole fucking.
I find no joy in it.

When he finally decided to act upon his desires to find other women, I withdrew.
Withdrew from all the social activities I formerly found fun.
I couldn't be around people.
All I wanted to do was cry.
And if I could keep myself from crying, I certainly wasn't engaged in the activity.
My friends want to know what is wrong.
Which would just make me want to cry.

How could I tell my friends that my husband was actively seeking other women?
I can't think of a way to say it without sobbing.
It is hard enough for me to deal with without having to tell my friends.

I am quiet at work.
I am quiet at conferences.
I teach and speak at conferences frequently.
I can rally to teach the things I know but once the session is over, I'm spent.
My once outgoing and warm personality is gone.
I have nothing to give anyone.
I have nothing inside me to share anymore.

I've taken to wearing black (even black nail polish).
I wish I could cover my face so no one could see my red-rimmed eyes.
It's not a fashion statement.
It is a reflection of the darkness within my heart.

I am in mourning.

24th – Grateful

On this day of thanks, I find myself reflecting upon the things I am thankful for in my life.
As we all do (or should).
I am grateful for:
- My health (I'm still alive after having melanoma 3 years ago).
- A successful business.
- The sunshine.
- The flowers.
- My sisters.
- My friends.
- Still having my parents.
- My smart & lovely daughter.
- My brilliant & handsome husband.

And finally,
The love of my husband.

Ah, there it is.

My husband loves me.
But wants the affection and sexual intimacy of other women.
He says he is not complete without this.
The total and complete bliss that once filled my heart and soul is gone.

I am so in love and would never tell him not to do what makes him happy.
He says it is like when he has other powerful experiences (i.e. public speaking, performing, etc.)
Well, to me, it most certainly is NOT the same.

On a mental level, I get it.
I get that he feels more energized by the experiences.

However, he may feel happier and fulfilled but I feel nothing but sadness and emptiness.
I am closed to him.
The happiness he wants to share with me is lost on me.
The walls around my heart that I willingly removed for him have returned.
Stronger and more impenetrable than ever before.

So what am I thankful for on this day of thanks?
I guess am grateful for still having defenses to protect my heart.
But really,
Nothing.

29th – Ceiling

I'm awake.
Staring at the ceiling.

I'm not sure what I hope to see there.
Certainly not an answer to my situation.
The situation that keeps me up at night.

Awake and thinking about how I feel.
Thinking about how to move.
   In any direction.

As my husband says, 'the genie is out of the bottle now'.
Which means, he has no intention of returning to the way things used to be.

The life that was blissful for me.
The love that felt safe.
The arms that felt comforting.
The lips that made me swoon.
The bare skin on skin that sent a thrill through my whole body.

So, no going back.
So, this means moving forward.
I don't know how to do it.
Take a step.
I try and get told I'm not safe.

Wait! What?
What do you mean, *I'M* not safe?

I'm the one stuffing all my feelings.
I'm the one taking a double dose of anti-depression meds.
I'm the one smiling while my heart breaks.

Swirling, whirling thoughts and emotions.
As I stare at the ceiling.

CHAPTER 3
Shrinking into Oblivion

DECEMBER

In this chapter, I try to look at things from a different perspective, hoping to find some understanding or relief from the pain. But it's to no avail. I'm shrinking, slowly but inevitably getting smaller every day.

Each imagined interaction of my husband with other women diminishes me further. I'm hiding, not just from everyone around me, but also from myself.

And yet, he tells me that I'm still number one.

It makes no difference. I'm dying inside, or at least wanting to.

His actions make it clear that I'm NOT his top priority, despite his empty words. Actions that I wasn't supposed to have any feelings or objections to.

There are moments of clarity when I realize that I would never be enough to fill the void inside him. At the time, I didn't understand that his emptiness as a narcissist needed to be filled constantly, and by everyone around him, including other women who didn't mean any more to him than I did.

In these pages, you'll witness my struggle to maintain a sense of self while being continually diminished by my husband's actions and words. You'll see me grappling with the realization that no matter what I do, I will never be enough for him.

I question everything I thought I knew about love, relationships, and my own self-worth.

2nd – Filters

I like to take pictures.
Lots of them (well, I used to but that's another story).
I rarely use filters since I like the natural colors of the world around me.

But I have a lot of communication filters that I've recently created for my husband.
Not because he asked for them, because they are just appearing.
The last few months, the communication between us has been breaking.
Not completely but in a few key places.
And it is spreading.
Like a, well, I don't know what but I find I have more filters each week.

Surprise Filter

As we sit at a table at a restaurant chatting with friends, you reach under the table and place your hand on my leg.
I jump imperceptibly; surprised at your small sign of affection.
I hope that you don't notice my surprise.
Simultaneously, my mind wanders to how you must do the same with your other woman.
I smile and realize that I'm not fully enjoying your love.
I shrink inside without being able to help it.

Gazing Filter

We have always had these sweet loving moments where we simply gazed at each other.

Across the room.
Sitting quietly next to each other.
Waking up and snuggling.
You whisper sweetly to me that you love me.
And then something creeps into me.
I wonder if you say the same thing to your other women.
My heart skips and shrivels just a bit.
The moment loses some of it's potency.
I've lost something that is sublime.
I hope you don't notice.

Skin Filter

There is nothing I love better than to run my fingers along your curves.
To appreciate the small of your back.
To hear you sigh when I lightly touch your collarbone.
To feel you relax when I stroke your cheek.
To press my naked breasts against your chest.
To feel your powerful legs.
But (isn't it always about the but?),
It only takes a few seconds and the moment of joy is gone.
I think about how they can do the same thing.
How they can appreciate your shape.
How they can enjoy your soft skin.
How they can make you sigh and moan.
I am lost.

Sex Filter

Sigh, to feel your desire for me.
The delightful sting of your pinching fingers.
Your strong grip on my wrists make me writhe and squirm.
It excites us both.

Your hard cock pressing against me.
My breathe coming faster as I become more aroused.
You whisper in my ear something about how you would play with me and one of them.
My breathe stops.
My heart stops.
My passion is tempered.
I want you.
I want you WITHOUT her in the room (real or imagined).
Even if they aren't there and you don't mention her, they are there in my mind.
I fight the tears.
Unless you spank me, then they flow freely.
I know you sense that the tears are more than the physical pain.
I know you want to free me from the bonds of my breaking heart.
But I know you do not realize the depth of my despair.
You enter me and I only can think of when you fuck them.
They are in the room.
The elephant in the room of my mind.
There is no letting go for me.
There is no pleasure for me.

-

All barriers (aka filters) became unknown with you.
Now, they are returning.
The barriers that I happily banished.
Return as strong as ever.
With reinforcements being added each day.
I want to tear them down so badly but I cannot.
I must protect myself.
And to protect myself from you is to lose the richest treasure I ever had.

9th – Coats Old and New

I'm here.
Waiting.

I wait each week for your return.
Only to find that you get here and want to leave again.
Leave to meet one of them.
And I feel like dirt.

Did you chose to not take me to the family event knowing that you would want to meet one of them afterwards?
Did you leave me here to watch our teenager knowing you didn't plan to come home?
Yes, that was your plan.

You say you care for me.
And when you say it, I believe you.
I'm beginning to wonder if I believe you
  Because I really want to
OR
  Because it's true.

What is it?
Truth.
The truth is you don't want me.
Not really.

Truth.
I'm here to care for your home.
Your child.
Your comfort.

Truth.
I don't keep you warm anymore so you need another one.
Or maybe I'm just the old coat to warm you when no one else will have you.

I feel like a old coat tossed aside.
And feeling pretty chilly myself.
I don't think I can spare any warmth for you.

Since I get no true warmth in return.

10th – Foolishness

I feel foolish right now
Foolish
I looked in your eyes I thought I saw love

I'm sure I saw your love
But it was fleeting.
It wasn't for me tonight.

Maybe it was for me for a few moments up for me.
Ultimately I don't know that it's actually love that you're sharing.
It might be love that you're sharing with me.
It might just be lust that you're sharing with her.

The bottom line is you've been gone for a week
And you came home tonight only to turn and leave again
To be in her arms not mine.

I guess I need to wake up
And realize

That I'm really not that important to you.

12th – In The Dark

I just want to be here
Here in the darkness
The darkness of the night

The darkness so I don't have to see anything
The darkness keeps me hidden
Darkness covers my despair

The darkness that keeps me hidden from you
The darkness that lets me hide
   From the sunshine of your smile
The darkness overwhelms the light that shone from within me
   The darkness that glistens for you

It's easier to be in the dark than to have my light extinguished
   Repeatedly
     Over and over and over again

By your false love

14th – Realization

It hits me
It hits me like a ton of bricks
I realize that I've loved a phantom
I loved an ideal
I've loved something that wasn't real

I have loved you
Let you have every bit of me
More of me that I've ever shared with anyone

My bad
I should've realized
The dream
The hope
The thing that all humans long for
Doesn't actually exist
Love
Love is a dream
You might have it for a moment
But that's all
The love that you have, it's a fantasy
It could never last

I realize now
That what we have is now a business deal
And I need to treat it as such
I need to let go of my childhood teenage fantasies
Of an all consuming love
I realize now it never existed

14th – Restless

Antsy
Edgy
All code for you wanting to go fuck someone else
I mean, let's be real
When you say that, that is what you mean
Don't try to kid me
I know the code now

Just say it:
    I want to be with one of them
    They are more exciting than having you
    You are old news
    You come with kid
    And responsibilities
    And baggage

    Never mind that you desire
    You desire my affection
    While I demand yours

Restless dick
That's what you are
I'm over it

16th – Circle

Feeling happy.
Feeling your love
Feeling your attention.
Letting myself swoon in your arms.
Warm
Cozy
Bliss

You whisper sweetly in my ear.
Murmurs of affection.

Then
One of them enters
Enters the room with your whisper.
"I'll be back later for you".

I feel like I got punched in the stomach.
The breathe leaves me.
I stop breathing to try and stop the hurt from spreading.
Too late.
It is throughout my body.
Frozen.
Now shallow breath.
A forced smile for your benefit.
A smile to try and make my soul believe it too.

I manage to keep the tears in check.
Until you leave.
Leave to go fuck one of them.
There is a roaring in my ears.

Tears burn my eyes.
I fall into the darkness.

Please!
Please, I beg the darkness
Please let me go.
Please let me leave this place of hell.
Hell couldn't be as bad as how this feels.
An all consuming pain.
Pain that sears through my heart.
That rips my soul apart and stomps it to pieces.

I self medicate with alcohol.
To ease the torture.
Ease my hopelessness
I try to sleep but stare at the ceiling
Trying to relax

Hoping you come home.
Whenever.
Hoping you don't come home.
Ever.

You will.
Eventually.
After you have fucked your way to satisfaction.
Fucked another with joy.
After you both had a good time.
While I sobbed with intolerable pain.

I'll be shut down.
And unwelcoming.
You'll caress me.

And whisper how exciting it was.
And how powerful you feel.

I want to share your joy.
I only feel agony.

You'll pay attention to me for a few days.
Attempt to make me feel loved.
My frozen and crushed heart will thaw and mend a bit.

Then one night, you'll whisper in my ear.
"I'll be back later for you"

And we start the cycle again.
The never-ending circle of joy and pain.

24th – No More

I love music.
All kinds of music.
I have an amazing amount of music in my iTunes library.
So much so that I leave my playlist on random so I can hear all of it.
A song came up last week that I hadn't heard in awhile.

I've always liked Annie Lennox and her work.
This song in particular has always had a poignant quality.
It struck me hard last week.

I'm so torn and distraught these past few years.
Desire
Despair
Desire
So many monsters.

I desire you, my husband.
I despair your desire for others, husband.
I desire your love, husband.

The monsters torment me.
When I look at you, I hear the words in my head.
No more "I love you's"
The language is leaving me
No more "I love you's"
The language is leaving me in silence.

Silence.
I choke on the words, "I love you".
My voice is gone.

I have no words.
No more words to tell you.
To tell you how despondent I am over your choice.
Your choice to share yourself intimately.
Sharing yourself in such a way that makes your touch less special.
Makes me less special.

Oh, so many monsters!
The demons haunt me.
I cannot say the words anymore.
Changes are shifting.
Inside and outside.

37st – Gagged

I'm trying.
Trying to embrace your choice.
Trying to be excited for your choice.
Trying not to sob over your choice.

Inasmuch, I suggested that we play together.
Play with one of them.
Together.

Maybe, just maybe
I can let go of the soul-crushing anguish
The debilitating apathy engulfing me.
If I can be a part of your experience.

I want to be excited.
I guess I am a bit.
Excited to wear your collar.
Excited to be your submissive.
Excited to be on display.
Excited to show my devotion.

But, I don't trust my voice.
I almost beg you to put the gag on me.
Your ownership is complete already.
But the collar and gag allow me to hide.

I know that sounds strange.
I'm naked, on display and flogged
And yet,

By not being able to speak,
I feel somehow hidden.

I'm not me in this moment.
I'm a body.
I'm the collar.
I'm the gag.

Thank you for silencing my heartache.

CHAPTER 4
The Ultimate Betrayal

JANUARY

In a desperate attempt to rationalize my husband's actions and make them more permissible, I agreed to join him for one of his rendezvous with a woman from his stable. I tried to be understanding, but this concession only pushed me deeper into depression.

He twisted my words around, making me the bad guy. I'm portrayed as the one who isn't enlightened enough to understand that what he was doing was just fine. Later, I learn that this manipulation tactic is called Blame Shifting, and he does it so well. I never stood a chance.

I withdraw even further into myself, setting alerts on my phone to remind me not to speak.

However, not speaking doesn't rid me of the distressing feelings inside. I don't want to feel like this, and no amount of suppressing my emotions makes me feel better. I find myself hoping my cancer comes back, giving me a reason to die. It seems like the only way to escape this suffering.

Unbeknownst to me, my husband starts yet another affair with one of his employees.

In this chapter, you'll witness the depths of my despair as I try to conform to my husband's twisted desires, only to be met with further betrayal. You'll see me grappling with the realization that no matter how much I try to understand and accommodate him, it will never be enough.

As I sink deeper into depression, you'll witness the dangerous thoughts that begin to consume me, and the desperate measures I consider just to escape the pain.

This is a raw and unfiltered look at the devastating impact of narcissistic abuse and the lengths a person will go to just to survive.

1st – Sharing Your Toy

I guess I'm grateful for your willingness to share.
Share one of them.
Meet one of them.
Experience one of them.
With you.

Your hope,
your desire
was to make it fun for all.
Especially for me.

I needed to show my submission.
Show my devotion
To you
My Master

Collared
Bound
Gagged
I became an observer.

And observe I did.
I saw you touch her.
Whisper to her.
Enjoy her.
Like a toy.

I got it.
She is a toy to you.
Yes, a person too

That you treat with respect.
That you consider her thoughts, feelings and boundaries.
You like her (but don't love)
But she is a toy nonetheless.

A toy that provides pleasure to you.
The pleasure of making her moan.
The pleasure of making her squirm.
The pleasure of making her wait.
For you.
To dominate.

As you teased her
You gazed at me.
You wanted me to feel
Your excitement
The thrill of having both of us

I wanna feel your fire
I wanna feel your joy
Let me blow your mind
I'm your sex toy

I didn't.
I wanted to but sadly not.
I felt many things but excitement wasn't one of them.

Your original toy fell down dark hole of despondency.
With no visible way to find the light again.

9th – Speak

I've been trying
Trying to be honest
Share my feelings
Mine
Not yours
My experience
How I feel
When you go fuck one of them for hours on end

I share
I'm calm (at least I try to be)
I'm logical
We discuss
How to move forward
How to stop the pain and frustration
On both sides

We end with no resolution
You want to fuck other women
I sob while you do so

You say, "go get a boyfriend"
I say I don't want one
I just want you
I want you to want to play with me
For hours on end

Instead, you play with me for minutes
After you fuck someone else for hours

Do I feel slighted?
Yes
Do I feel less than worthy?
Yes
You can say I'm insecure
I don't believe so
My feelings are valid.

I guess the easiest thing is not to speak

9th – Crossing the Streams

You've been having your fun
Fun with one of them
While I feel utter despair
But at least, it's been private

Private lives
Have stayed private
Separate
They are toys
To be played with
Respected yes
But played with by you
At a hotel
A suitable place for your play

Our lives
Are ours
No disruption
No intrusion
To our, or their
Privacy

Sure, they have families
Husbands
As we have a family
Our home
Is our sanctuary
A (kinda) safe place for us
Our family

The serenity not encroached upon
With anything other than your absence
And words

But now,
You and one of them have crossed the streams
You went to a home
I objected
It didn't matter
You said I was illogical
Her family was gone
Her husband knew you were there
To play
With his wife

Your rationale;
Three adults didn't care
It was just a house
Even mind that it is THEIR house
The house that THEIR family (and kids)
Is safe and happy (I guess) in.

The delicate balance of our universe has been disrupted
Again
It was already on the edge
You don't care that I care
That you fucked her in THEIR house
That you know her better
After being at THEIR house

You don't need to know them better
They must remain toys

Their private lives must remain theirs
If you want to maintain the outwardly appearing fragile calm of our universe

In the words of the great Dr. Egon Spengler:
This is bad.
Imagine all life as you know stopping instantaneously
And every molecule in your body
Exploding at the speed of light
Total plutonic reversal
That's bad.

This is bad.

10th – Won't Go Away

Despite the very ambiguous meaning of the lyrics, this song is emotionally powerful.

These feelings won't go away

I want them to.
But they never seem to

You know it ain't easy for these thoughts here to leave me

You know the sorrow
Is always present
In my heart
But you continue on the path

Diamonds they fade

Just like the bright
Blissful
Enduring
Diamond of our love

They been knocking me sideways
They been knocking me out lately

Knocking out my zeal
My enthusiasm
My fire for life
My passion for you

I keep thinking in a moment that time will take them away

I know you hope
As I do
That I will come
To feel as you do

And I'm telling you
But these feelings won't go away

11th – Open

Opening
My heart
My soul
The soft, squishy and vulnerable part of me
To you

I opened
Everything
My thoughts
My desires
To you

Somehow you knew what I was hiding
Deep inside
You opened yourself
Your thoughts
Your desires
To me

We unbolted the castle walls
Built so carefully
Over the years
Our essence
Given freely
Willingly
Despite the rust that had formed upon the locks

Inside
The most precious treasures
Awaited us both

The blissful love
Amongst the warm and safe cushions
Of each other's arms and lips

Openness
Wonderful
Special
Elusive for so many

Then
You slammed the door
On yourself
Your choice
Withdrew your access
To the soft vulnerable part
Deep inside me

Stunned
I found myself cold
Without you
To reach inside me

What was open
Is now closed

18th – Games

It's a fun game
One of us travels
And you give instructions
For me to follow

Instructions
Designed to spur our imaginations
To excite
And connect
Us both over the miles

The game
Is not interesting
To me
Currently

You play games
With one of them too
Without telling me
And I wonder
Why
Why you didn't tell me
Why I had to ask
If you were with one of them

I don't like wondering
I don't like having to ask repeatedly
Why you don't respond
To my messages
Especially when we had

Spoken of connecting
On FaceTime
That evening
To connect us over the time zones

You act like
It's no big deal
You are open
About your fun
And games with them
And believe that all
You need to do
Is show me a little attention
And all will be well

The game is no longer fun
I'm out of tears
Listless
And empty

17th – Isolation

We move through the universe
Among others
Seeking
A human connection
But end up
Feeling
Empty
And alone

Many say
That we come into world alone
And leave it equally alone
I believe
That we come here
With so many others
Seeking
Connectedness
Feeling it
And quickly finding
That we
Are the center
Of our own universe

Our experience
Occasionally
Let's us feel connected
But ultimately
We are alone

Alone
To feel our own
Mortality
To feel so alone

In our experience

21st – Recurrence

It's sad
But I hope for recurrence.
Recurrence of my cancer.
So I can escape the misery
Of my current experience

There are different types of recurrence:
Local means that the cancer has come back in the same place.
    This seems unlikely for me
    Since they hacked a giant chunk out
Regional means that the cancer has come back in the lymph nodes near the original location.
    Since my cancer had a high rate of replication, I suppose this could happen.
Distance means the cancer has come back in another part of the body.

I can tell you that, once you have cancer, every time you get an ache, you worry.
I don't worry a lot
But it does cross my mind
When I get an abnormal mammogram
I'm scared
When I get a bad flu
I worry about my lungs

The bottom line for me is this: I want the cancer to come back.
I want to end this misery
The misery of feeling like death
The tears that come
From feeling

Alone
Cast aside
  Like an old coat
Empty
  Of passion
  Of life
Or just numb
Because the pain is too great to bear

Recurrence
Thou name is hope
For relief

CHAPTER 5
The Numbness of Survival

FEBRUARY

I'm shutting down, walking through each day in a daze. I pretend that life is wonderful with my wolf in sheeps clothing, but the reality is far from it. I'm trapped in a situation that I have no idea how I got into or how to escape.

My husband's insistence that I'm important rings hollow. I've come to realize that I'm just another 'source' for his excessive need for attention and admiration. My feelings and opinions don't amount to anything as far as he is concerned. Nothing really changes, no matter how much I express my discontent.

Witness the numbness that takes over as I try to navigate my daily life. You'll see me going through the motions, putting on a brave face for the world while inside, I'm crumbling.

I'll take you through the realization that my husband's words are empty, and that I'm merely a tool for his own gratification. You'll feel the helplessness and despair as I come to terms with the fact that my voice holds no weight in this relationship. All while beginning to glimpse the void inside him that constantly needs new sources of energy.

This is a chapter about survival, about the ways in which we shut ourselves down just to make it through another day, even in the face of unimaginable emotional abuse.

1st – Damned If I Do

Why?
Why do I feel so hopeless?
It just isn't like me.
To be apathetic.

My requests feel
Reasonable
To me
But not to you.

If I make a request
You shut me down
By saying that it is arbitrary
My whim
Without reason

I promise you
That any request I make
Is most definitely NOT arbitrary

Your decision to disregard
My request
Feels, well, just more than a little condescending
You say you hear me
But your response
Is patronizing at best

Why do I bother?
To make any request?
A request that may help me

Feel more cared for
Considered

So, I stop
I shut down my requests
And pretend
Pretend that all is well
When it is not

You have no idea
Except for the rare time
That some unhappiness
Leaks out of my
Carefully constructed facade

The problem is
That when I shut down
Any dialogue
That I have interest
In discussing
Due to your superiority
I shut down
My love too
At least a portion of it

I don't want to shut down
Or shut you out
But your smugness of
Being right (which makes me wrong)
Leaves me feeling as if I have no choice

What do you want?
Because this isn't working for me
Anymore
And you don't seem to care
If it works now or ever
And I feel damned
Regardless of the
Direction I take

So the choice is yours now
I give it to you

23rd – Vive la Difference

We are so very different.

I've thought a lot about
Myself
And how I feel about
Myself
Fucking others

When I have been physical with someone
In the past
I was seeking connection
Intimacy
That wonderful thing that all humans desire

For you, fucking other women
You say it is not a substitute for me
You say that it isn't the sex
That's special
It is me that is special
And what makes having sex with me
Special
Nothing
Nobody can be a substitute for me

Your activities with other people
Don't take away
From how you are with me
Just another
And different
Facet of your life

When you go off
To fuck one of them
I feel left out
And useless
Miserable

Knowing you are having sex
Developing an intimate relationships elsewhere
Feels bad
Very bad
Like something is missing for you
And you need someone else
To fulfill you

Our relationship is lessened
And breaking
Along with my heart

I don't know the answer
To our dilemma
To our differences

CHAPTER 6
The Breaking Point

MARCH

My husband tells me to go find a boyfriend. I don't want to, but he insists, saying he wants to be proud of me pleasing someone other than him. I later discover that this was a ploy to turn against me if I ever objected to his infidelity again. I try to rally myself to comply, but I cannot. It's not in me. It never was.

After years of feeling joyless, for I have nothing to feel joy about, I'm apathetic to my condition. Living like this constantly is tiring and boring.

I'm starting to see how I have to make a decision. Something *HAS* to change, and it appears I'm the one who needs to do it. I'm still trapped financially after following his instructions to quit my VP job two years ago.

I decide. We must part. And he says no. We cannot.

I'm back where I started, still searching for an answer between crying jags.

In this chapter, you'll witness the breaking point, the moment when I finally realize that something has to give. You'll see me grappling with the realization that I'm the one who needs to take action, even as my husband continues to manipulate and control me.

I'll take you through the heartbreaking decision to leave, and the resistance I face from my husband. You'll feel the desperation and hopelessness as I find myself back at square one, searching for a way out.

This is a chapter about the struggle for autonomy, about the fight to reclaim one's life in the face of overwhelming opposition. It's a testament to the courage it takes to even consider leaving an abusive relationship.

2nd – Honoring You Sir

I adore you Sir
My wish
Is for you to be happy
Powerful
Realizing your potential
Happily seeing you
Make your mark
In the world

I wish to honor you
Honor the power
And brillance
Inside you
And, excite you
by submitting all
And pushing past
My fears
To find the reward
Of pleasing and exciting you

If I was to
Have sex with others
It would be
A way to please you
To honor you
By doing something
You commanded
That pushed me
I would be like having sex with you by proxy

I wouldn't want it unless you were there
Instructing me
Protecting me
Keeping me close and safe

I would do these things
To excite you
To show the world
(or at least a small portion of it)
How we have
Built a relationship
On trust
And enduring love

I would feel my heart
Swell
With pride
As you watch me
Watch me
Submit to your
Desires
While seeing the fire
In your eyes
That burn into me
Marking me
Making me yours
Forever

8th – Boring

Are you bored?
Reading
Repeatedly
About
  Misery
  Sadness
  Emptiness
  Despair

I can tell you
That I'm even tired of it
Tired of feeling this way
Tired of crying
Or trying not to

I suppose that
Is why
I avoid my friends
I don't want them to
Be as bored
As I am
With my tears
And long face

They say you shouldn't withdraw
But
When I'm close to tears

I don't
Want to be
Around my
Friends
Burdening them
With my woes

I'm also ashamed
Ashamed
Of my husband's choice
His choice
That feels like
I'm inadequate
While being
A doormat
I'm ashamed
For choosing
To allow him to hurt me
To my core

Yes, it is my choice
And the poly world would tell me
That I don't have to choose

That I should

Either

Be jumping for joy for his desires

OR

Divorce

Gee, that was helpful
Not much of a choice
And oh, such a bore

10th – Teetering

Something has changed in me.
A choice
Is pending
The choice is mine

Resignation
Despair
Hopelessness
Emptiness

To shut down
My sadness
And become
One of 'those' women
That stay because they
Don't know what else to do
With themselves
And cannot conceive of a blissful
All consuming love like ours again

OR

Let you go
Be who you say you are
Let you go with love
For I love you too much
To hold you from
What you say is your happiness

I'm teetering
On this balance beam
You sense
That something
Has changed
But I remain silent
While sensing the abyss
On either side of me

I feel a quietness inside
A patience
While I wait for the answer
Wait for guidance

At the same time
I feel a ferociousness
To be consumed
And to consume you
To hold and clutch something
So precious
So special
I could never hope
To realize it again
And to say goodbye

13th – Nemesis

Down a Wikipedia rabbit hole
I land upon the goddess Nemesis
I always find
Learning
About Greek gods and goddesses
Fascinating
Along with the ties that bind them together

Now I read The Fall of the House of Cabal
The story is about
The nemesis
And subsequent testing
Of each character
By each unique nemesis

All of a sudden
I'm struck
What is my nemesis?
The universe
Has placed this
Pause for reflection
Smack in front of me
As if to slap me with a halibut*

Nemesis,
The winged balancer of life,
Dark-faced goddess,
Daughter of Justice,
Portrayed as a winged goddess

Wielding a whip or a dagger.
The distributor of fortune
neither good nor bad
simply proportion
to what is deserved.
Nemesis corrects any disturbance
To its correct proportion,
justice will not pass unpunished.

What is my nemesis?
What 'correcting' do I need?
What is deserved?
Apparently
I have created a disturbance
Within my universe
Within our universe?

By offering to remove myself
From limiting your happiness
Or your choice
To explore
The flesh of other women
Will not silence
The disturbance
Will not keep me from being punished (at least, not in a fun way)

I suppose I must deserve this
By creating this test
Allowing my life
My happiness
To be between two sorrowful choices

Nemesis is my closest companion
And will not let me rest
For even one moment

*You'll have to read the Johannes Cabal series to appreciate that line.

17th – Illusion of Choice

Trembling
I chose to tumble down the abyss
To a place
Of sadness
Yet full of love
And acceptance
I strove
To care for us both

My choice
I let you go with love
To the place
That you say
Is required
For your happiness

I did not present this
As an ultimatum
But my choice
To love
And care
For myself
And you
By removing
Myself
From the constant pain
And anguish

Your immediate reaction to my choice
Was to say 'no'
Faced with my choice
My decision
To love you
And let you go
You choose
To drag me out of the chasm
You say you would be unhappy
Without me

A few days later
You say you still need this
This physical outlet
Of sexual intimacy
Without me
To feel whole
And fully yourself

My choice
My attempt
Of self-care
Is now moot
My choice
Becomes no choice
I have become
One of 'those'
Expected to sit silently
Weeping
While you 'explore'
Yourself
In the arms of other women

As I sense the safety
And warmth
I feel for you
Ebb away
Along with my
Passion for living
I am a shell
Hosting the shadow
Of a once
Great and powerful woman

26th – For What It's Worth

For what it's worth
I love you
For what is worse
I really do

I love you too much
To say no
To hold you you down

Please come back
Embrace our loving
And the warm bed
That makes us feels alright

Things happens
And we have fun
And love
Until it the morning comes

For what it's worth
I love you
Adore you
Do anything for you

Now it's time
To love us both
Enough to release you
And myself
From the pain
That holds us both

I return to the land
That owns me
You return to
The desire to have
All women
That controls you

Hopefully
We find peace
In two different
Locations
And find the things
That are worth our time
And love

CHAPTER 7
The Line in the Sand

APRIL

I make another decision. I decide that I cannot have sex with my husband if he wants to have sex with other women. It is a scary declaration, but I have to do it in order to care for myself. I'm desperately trying to care for myself. Not to mention he won't get tested for STDs (I did for my own peace of mind).

I'm cold and alone, unable to breathe and show myself to anyone.

My husband now has at least five women (that I know of) that he 'regularly' has sex with. I'm no longer one of them. I can't do it. It is a gut-wrenching realization that I can no longer bear his touch. The thought of him touching me makes me want to vomit.

I feel robbed of my happiness. He is the thief. I let him love-bomb me. I beging to the realize that I walked willingly into this nightmare.

You'll feel the desperation as I try to hold onto my sanity, even as everything around me feels like it's crumbling.

I had the courage to assert a boundary, even as I was gripped by fear and isolation.

This is a chapter about self-preservation, about the moments when we finally say "enough" and start fighting for ourselves in the darkest of times.

This chapter marks a turning point, a moment when the scales begin to fall from my eyes, and I start to see the situation for what it truly is. It's a harrowing journey, but one that was necessary if I was ever to find my way back to myself.

5th – Don't Touch Me

You can touch them
OR
You can touch me

Your choice

When you touch me after touching them
I cringe
When you kiss me after kissing them
I want to vomit

So, you've chosen.
Their touch is more important than mine.
So be it.

5th – Life Without Air

Feeling tense
Only shallow breath
Allows me to contain
The emotions
Pent up
Inside

Without air
There is no breath
No ability to speak
No ability for the words
To come tumbling out
The anguish
Suppressed

Apparently,
This is called the
"freeze or faint"
response to danger
Or a giant grizzly

I am in danger
Danger of letting
The damaged
And battered
Little girl hiding
Deep inside
Get hurt

I stuff down
And suffocate
The girl
And keep her
Under lock and key
Not listening to her pain

I can't help her
So I crush
The air supply
And keep us both
Drifting without air

6th – Elephant In The Room

You whisper
How much fun you had
You want
Me to be excited
By your NRE
You want my compersion

Whelp, I can't give you want I don't have.

You bring them to OUR bed
With your whispers
Of desire
Desire for me
Because you got off with one of them

By bringing them to our bed
You demote me
To nothing
Nothing that matters
Because you are thinking
Of your fuck
With them
And not me

Even if you don't mention one of them
They is always present
In our bed
In our home
When you touch my flesh

Because I feel
That you are desiring them
But I'm the closest thing at hand

Yes, a thing
That is what I feel like
I know you don't get it
You don't get how
Crushed
Obliterated
Forlorn
I can be over your choice
To allow one of them
Or any other woman
Be sexually intimate with you

I pray your happy with this choice
Because it is killing me
At least one of us
Can be happy
And sexually fulfilled

Even if we pretend it isn't happening
You fawn over me
And I stiffly smile
They are all still the elephants in the room

7th – Thief

A thief in the night
Has robbed me of
The passion I have
For my husband

Well, the passion
Is still within me
I feel a burning desire
When I look at him
Wanting
To feel his strong hands
Upon my soft flesh
Owning me

Then I freeze
Remembering the pain
When I experience his touch
His kisses
Leaving me nauseous

The blissful
Floating
That I sense
When he 'swoons' me
Is gone
Hijacked
By his choice

His choice
To pursue
Intimacy
In other women
Has shut down
One of the most special
Things we shared

No longer
Special
My touch
Kiss
Snuggle
Fuck
Just like any other

Demoted
To just another fuck
I feel swindled
Our sweet love
Embezzled
By my husband
And given to one of them
Or any other skirt
He desires

So now
We are partners
Without intimacy
Roommates

That share a bed
(and warmth)
But no sex

Can I put the thief in jail?
The sad part, is no.
The thief cannot return
The broken happiness

16th – Endless Cycle of Pain

Perfect
Our love
Our bliss

EXCEPT
This
This 'need' you have
To fuck other women

Thank you for being
Honest
Even if I'm still
Off-balance
After getting poly-bombed

You found another one
And now you go
To try 'her'
The one
That somehow
Fulfills you
Or some 'need'
You say you have

I stay home
Sobbing
Too tired to rage anymore
Searching
For a hole

Deep enough to bury
My pain

You return
Renewed
Rejuvenated
Exhilarated
Reaching for me
I cringe
Your desire
Has been enflamed
By 'her'
My desire
Has been eliminated
By 'her'

Using all the strength
I can muster
I attempt
To stuff
The desolation
The barren
Wasteland
Of misery

Tears threaten
To leak out
I awkwardly smile at you
And curl up
While you hold me
Tightly
And I reach

For the escape
Of sleep to take
The pain away

You say that she
Is just a friend
With benefits
Not your wife
Your love

I know you love me
And I you
I start to thaw
Relax
As we express
Our love
And devotion
To each other

Then
It comes
Again
Your 'need'
The 'need' to fuck one of them
And off you go
To have a good ole time
While I'm demoted
And crushed
To nothing
Again

The cycle starts
Bruising
Our love
Again

I can't help
But wonder
How many cycles do we have left?

24th – Survivor

The ugly
Scary
C word

Cancer
There
I said it

It came
To visit
Three years ago

I was lucky
I saw it
Early
And it was hacked
Out of my body

I have scars
That I own
I own the fact
That I'm a survivor

I survived cancer
I can survive your "need"
To fuck other women
To minimize me
And my uniqueness

To reduce
My total adoration of you
To nothing

I hope I can survive your betrayal and lies

25th – Intruder

I hear everything you say, Sir
My head gets it
But my heart
Not so much

You let one of them in OUR home.
I NEVER want to see 'her' again
I NEVER want 'her' near my child
I NEVER want to speak to 'her'
'She' will NEVER be admitted into my family
'She' will NEVER be my friend
'She' is NEVER welcome in my home
EVER

'She' is an intruder
'She' has embedded herself
In your pants (pun intended)
You don't get to fuck me too
You don't get to reach my deepest consciousness

Your loss because I'm amazing

The poly-elitists would say
I'm horribly insecure and have loads of baggage
How is that any different from anyone in this world"
I'm wonderful and sure of myself
It is you that are the insecure one with 'needs'
To bring an intruder into our lives
To make yourself feel whole

28th – Mask

Getting through each day
Became a chore
Putting on my makeup
Along with a calm and happy mask

Wearing a mask wears you out.
Faking is fatiguing.
The most exhausting activity is pretending to be what you know are you know you aren't.
- Rick Warren

Yes, I'm worn out
Faking my acceptance
Pretending to be happy
For my husband
To fuck other women

Each time he goes
To his one of his Metamors*
Another little piece of me
Dies
And my mask becomes
Stronger
Tougher
Becoming armor
To protect all of me
From him

I don't like it
It is very tiring

I don't like faking my happiness
Or stuffing my sorrow
I'm tired of pretending to be ok

I'm not ok
I'm suffering
Higher doses of meds
Just numb me

Where did the
Happy
Joyful
Amazing
Woman that embraces life passionately go?

I want her back
I want her to stop meds
I want her to smile
When the sunshine
Warms her face
Instead of her mask

*Metamor isn't even a word in the dictionary, just another word the poly world made up to justify their choices.

CHAPTER 8
The Numbness of Despair

MAY

Content warning: This chapter contains references to suicidal thoughts.

I've reached the point where I don't care anymore. I probably do somewhere, in the place where I've buried my feelings, but I give up. You get your way while I wear a mask every day.

Even while being resigned, I'm angry in some way, still trying to make sense of how polyamorists can hurt so many people. I later discover that this was a convenient ruse that my husband used to be unfaithful. All the polyamorists I know say that his behavior was absolutely NOT how they treat those they care about.

It is obvious I've given up while not giving up. I'm trying to establish boundaries for myself, for my mental health, since I feel my sanity slipping away.

At the end of the month, I make the discovery that I'm suicidal. For the first time in my life. I should be scared, but I don't care.

Unbelievable as it is, there is the moment when I reach the end of my rope and find myself contemplating the unthinkable. You'll see the numbness that comes with total resignation, the sense of having lost the battle.

I'll take you through the anger and confusion as I try to make sense of my husband's actions, and the way he has manipulated the concept of polyamory to justify his infidelity. You'll feel the struggle as I continue to try to establish boundaries, even as I feel my grip on reality slipping.

This is a chapter about the darkest of thoughts, about the moment when death seems like the only escape from an unbearable situation. It's a testament to the insidious nature of emotional abuse, and the way it can erode one's will to live.

I grapple with the realization that I am suicidal, and the strange calm that comes with no longer caring about my own life. It's a disturbing and heart-wrenching revelation, but one that ultimately serves as a wake-up call.

Please know that if you are having thoughts of suicide, you are not alone. Help is available. Consider reaching out to a trusted friend, family member, therapist, or a suicide prevention hotline in your area.

1st – Resignation

I guess
This is the place
Where all monogamists
That love polyamorists
Get to eventually
I concede
You win

This place
Allows for love
To anesthetize pain
Torment numbed
By being repeated
Again and again
Over time

I don't get it
Don't get your 'need'
To fuck other women
Or anyone
Other than me
I don't know
That I ever will

I feel small
Diminished
And not longer able
To acknowledge
The deep
And lasting

Hurt I feel
Each time
You go to one of them

I'm just too tired
Drained
There are no more tears
To shed
My grief
In losing the relationship
We had that was so perfect
And lovely

You say you feel no different
About me
And I still adore you
Now, I am
A shell

No more tears
No more rage
No more meds
No more intimacy
No more opening my heart
To a place only you could reach

Just resignation
That to be with you
Means I must have to
Smile
And carry on

2nd – The Chains That Bind

"I will break the chains that bind me, happiness will find me. Leave the past behind me, today my life begins."
-- Yao

Polyamorists regard monogamy as:

- Unrealistic
- Unnatural
- Contradicts human biology
- Cause emotional trama
- Defies modernity
- A waste of time
- Self sacrificing
- Possessive
- Ancient monolith

While polyamory is:

- Our natural state
- Love and sexual attraction are things we can't control
- More evolved
- More enlightened
- Freedom to love
- No rules
- No one definition
- More satisfying
- Better for children (it takes a tribe...)
- Is an orientation (no different than LBGT)

With all that against monogamy, why even consider it?
Because
Polyamory is delusional
And selfish at best.

Polyamorists can throw off the
Chains that bind
- Religion
- Social norms

But by doing so
Polyamorists walk into
A different kind of bondage
The chains of your sexual desires.
The addiction of chasing the all-powerful NRE*

"Thrills come at the beginning and do not last.
If you decide to make thrills your regular diet and try to prolong them artificially, they will all get weaker and weaker and fewer and fewer and you will be a bored, disillusioned old man [or woman] for the rest of your life."
-- C.S. Lewis

Polyamorists are NOT actually free
Freedom is found in self-governance and self-control
NOT doing whatever the hell you want

All human beings desire being in love
The connection that starts off exciting
And thrilling
The breathlessness isn't often sustained over time
It doesn't die

It is alive
Grows
Matures

This peaceful love allows for a deeper connection
A true freedom
To explore the world
Knowing that your deep and rich connection is constant
A connection that can never be replaced
By NRE* (or a different fuck)

*"This quieter love is a deep unity, maintained by the will and deliberately strengthened by habit.
Reinforced by grace, it enables a couple to keep their promises.
It is on this love that the engine of marriage is run: being in love was the explosion that started it."*
-- C.S. Lewis

The profound and intense love
Connection and tranquility
With my husband
Has been blasted to bits
And he is now chained
To his choice

* New Relationship Energy

3rd – Decision

My beloved,

I've made a decision.

I have decided that no matter what, I adore you and am yours. I am your wife and partner for always. I will never abandon you.

That said, I am removing any 'rules' I may have requested previously regarding your need to seek intimacy elsewhere. I may not be happy about it but I can't continue this way. I have chosen to be free of pain. You are free. Free to see whomever and do whatever you wish whenever you desire because I know you need this freedom. You have no limits from me anymore.

I may not be able to give you every piece of my heart and body right now but I want you to know I adore you nonetheless. I know this won't be for always because of our love for each other.

Always your devoted wife

5th – Cake

I wondered if polyamory was simply a nice way of saying, 'I get to fuck around and come back to you and a home-cooked meal?'

Was this a community of cake eaters who weren't willing to put what little energy they had left at the end of the day into one relationship?

Was I, along with all the multiple relationship types, afraid of too much intimacy with one person
 or just convinced that monogamy was the road to sexual death?

These questions are not mine
They are from a self-identified polyamorist
If she is asking herself these questions, why is it so wrong for others to wonder those things about her or other polyamorists?
When I read these statements, I can almost hear Jeff Foxworthy saying:

You might be an intimacy-phob…
if you are convinced monogamy is sexual death

You might be a smug poly-elitist snob…
if you want your partner to stay home while you wallow in the NRE of your latest Friend With Benefits

You might be greedy and unrealistic…
if you want your cake and eat it too

We can also have statements like this if you are the monogamist in the relationship:

*You might be a self-sacrificing, co-dependent martyr…
if you sit miserably at home with the kids while your partner has an exciting date night with someone else.*

*You might be a possessive, insecure, unenlightened, dysfunctional prude…
if you want to spend the little free time you have with your spouse.*

I would say that none of these are correct, but then again, some of them or parts of them, just might be. There is a lot of gray area.

And lastly, as Marie Antoinette infamously said, 'Let them eat cake" and was shortly thereafter sentenced to death on the guillotine for the crime of treason (poly-bombed monogamists feel like their partner is treasonous for wanting sex with others).

Cake anyone?

7th – Fairness

I haven't been fair
To you
Or myself

I've diminished the value
Of them
To you and your
Sense of freedom
Because of my need to have
Your warmth and affection

You give it to me
Often and freely
But my sense of
Partnership and love
Is threatened
When you go to one of them
For something that is missing here
What is it?

You feel (I'm guessing)
Resentful
When I question your choice
To express your independence
While my need for trust
And assurance
Feels wholly and utterly rejected

It is fair to either of us
To feel this way?
Fair is a squishy word
And perceptions of fair can vary

Was it fair of you to drop
   The poly-bomb on me
Was it fair of me to react
   With anger and anguish?
Was it fair of you to go to one of them
   Directly after returning from a week-long business trip?

Was it fair for me to insist you that you never go

   To 'her' home or meet 'her' husband/family?

All the 'requests' I've made
To protect my heart
And the blissful life I have with you
Have failed
And you don't understand
My needs or motivations
For attempting to set those boundaries

So, in the spirit of fairness
I give you carte blanche
To do whatever you desire
With whomever you desire
Whenever you desire
Your desire for freedom and independence
Is yours to explore
And now I am removing myself

From the sphere of pain
By removing your access
To my heart and body

I am no longer yours
To have and to hold
I don't know that I can wear your collar
Nor should I call you Master
If I can't give you all of me
I will be present in the room
I will care for our child
I will care for our home
I will care for our business
But the important, precious and special parts of me
Belong to only me now
You've shut the door on yourself

Is that fair to you?
Or me?
It's never that easy and now,
Fairness isn't a part of it anymore

13th – Collar

I 'removed' the collar
You had placed on me
It couldn't remain
When I couldn't give you
All of me
It didn't feel honorable
To wear it
While I constructed
Obstacles to protect myself
From you

The collar symbolized my ultimate
Commitment
Love
And devotion to you
And while I am still
Committed
Love
And devoted to you
There are parts of me
That are no longer yours

When I told you this
You became angry
Stating that I
Was dismantling
Our very special relationship

How?
I ask
How do I care for myself?
How can I be honest with you about my feelings?
How can I protect my heart while I adjust to the choice you have made?
How do I adapt to the new status of our relationship you have chosen?

I do NOT want
- To shut you out
- To merely warm your bed
- To no longer feel the extraordinary physical connection when we made love
- To build a barricade around my soul
- To withdraw from the incredibly unique and breathtaking passion and bliss we have with each other
- To remove the collar

I will fully submit to you again
One day
And be able to wear your collar
With self-confidence and delight
For us both

Just not today

18th – What's In It For Me?

I'm part of a Yahoo group
A group that is made up of monogamous people
With polyamorous partners
We share
Our struggles
And successes
But mostly struggles
With our partners choice

A question came up recently
That made me think
About my situation

What's in it for me?

What benefit do I get from my husband
   Getting to have a FWB?
What benefit does my daughter get from her father
   Having another sexual partner other than her mother?
What benefits does our family unit realize from his choice?

At this point, I can plainly state: none
There have been no benefits
For anyone
In this household
Except
He gets to have a few hours of sexual fun and games very week

The rest of the time
Our house is filled with
Angst (her)
Anger (her)
Anxiety (me and her)
Apathy (me)
Cranky (her)
Depression (me)
Detachment (me)
Despair (me)
Frustration (him)
Fulfillment (him after a date)
Giddy (him after a date)
Grief (me)
Heartbroken (me)
Hopelessness (me)
Impatient (him)
Irritated (her)
Isolation (me)
Pain (me)
Passionate (him after a date)
Rebellion (her)
Sadness (me and her)
Shutdown (me)
Suicidal (me)
Tense (me)
Resentment (him)
Withholding (me)

Sounds like so much fun, doesn't it?
I'm glad he is having fun because it sucks for the rest of us.

I feel like my home is being blasted apart
All because he HAS to have sex with other women.

What's in it for us?

All the feelings above.
And sadly, I don't see that changing anytime soon.

25th - MIA

I ask myself
"What is missing?"
From our relationship
From being an amazing woman
From being present
From my life

I have removed myself
From the very intimate
And loving connection
That we shared

At the very minimum
I'm missing the passion
Of living
But I'm also missing my libido
Something that has never left me
And has historically been very high

Each day
I wake up
Determined to be

- happy
- grateful
- carefree
- focused
- productive

- loving
- relaxed
- content
- passionate
- secure
- open

And very day I wake up and find all of those things missing-in-action

CHAPTER 9
The Futile Coping Mechanisms

JUNE

As I attempt to minimize the other women, I reduce them to mere labels. It's another way that I try to find sense in the senselessness that is my life.

My moods swing wildly. I work to keep my mouth shut, and yet the ugly things come out nonetheless. I'm hurting. I want him to feel the hurt, to at least acknowledge the excruciating pain I feel each waking moment.

I feel the sands of time slipping away, along with my sanity. It's my fault. All my fault. (His way of twisting my reality - I later learn this is called gaslighting, and he's good at it.)

I'm desperate in my attempts to cope with an impossible situation. You'll see me trying to minimize the impact of my husband's infidelity, to reduce his partners to labels in an effort to make the situation more bearable.

I'll take you through the wild mood swings, the constant battle to hold my tongue even as the pain demands to be expressed. You'll feel the anguish of wanting my husband to understand, to acknowledge the depth of my suffering.

This is a chapter about the mental gymnastics we perform to maintain control in the face of chaos.

You'll read about the insidious effects of gaslighting, as I start to internalize the blame, to believe that everything is my fault.

This chapter is a portrayal of the futile coping mechanisms we employ when faced with narcissistic abuse. It's a reminder that these strategies, while understandable, ultimately do not serve us.

It's a difficult chapter, one that lays bare the psychological toll of being in a relationship with a narcissist. But it's also a necessary step in the journey, a clear-eyed look at the reality of the situation, before healing can begin.

1st – Satisfaction

Sure, I'm still trying
Trying to come to terms
With the choice you've made

The choice that makes me small
The choice that tells me that I don't matter
The choice that shows me that my feelings are meaningless
The choice that indicates that I'm not exciting
The choice that lets me know that I'm truly unimportant
To you

Well, sure
You can have your cake
And I'll let you 'have' me
But you will NOT get any satisfaction from it

You MAY get to fuck me
BUT
You will NOT get an orgasm from me
(Not that I've been able to feel passion or anything that passes for desire for almost a year now and I can't remember the last time I had an orgasm.)

You may need me to satisfy your male ego
That you can satisfy me
And your other FWBs
Forget it.
I'm keeping my satisfaction to myself
Get your ego strokes from them.
(pun intended)

Never
Ever
As long as you want to do so with some other female
You don't deserve satisfaction from me
I'm not your FWB
I'm your wife
And I am devoted to you
But you don't get the satisfaction of knowing that you can please me
EVER

7th – Trigger Finger

Triggered
Again
You say you are restless and I flip out
I've been quietly going about my business
   And keeping my mouth shut
Feeling pretty good
Not great but not like death
   Or wanting to die

I said horrible things
I wanted to hurt you
I wanted you to feel as miserable
   and be in as much agony as I
I couldn't seem to stop myself
All my filters were gone
It was awful

I'm so sorry for my outburst
However, I realize that I'm not sorry for all of it
I was sorry for my tone and intent.
   My tone was one of rage and so very ugly
   My intent was to hurt you.
I was NOT sorry for telling you how I felt
   But how it was delivered along
   And my choice of words

When we are cuddly, snuggly and affectionate
   We are truly in that moment and blissfully happy
Life feels wonderful and so very special with you
I feel that way about everything we share

I genuinely adore you
   Love doing little things to please you
   Make you feel special

The switch gets flipped
   When I realize I'm not special
  Again
You say that what makes being intimate special is me
   I really, really hear you in my head
   But I really, really don't feel it in my heart
When we get intimate
   I'm so happy
   But
   Inevitably
   I realize that what we are sharing is not unique
   Or special
   I struggle to stay in that moment fully.
I so miss being able to fully give you everything
Despite everything I've tried to do for myself
I'm still triggered
This feeling sits in my soul like a disease

11th – OSO or Metamour or FWB or Booty Call

Metamour = Other Love
OSO = Other Significant Other
FWB = Friend With Benefits
Booty Call = Sexual Rendezvous

All of these involve another person
That is involved with your partner

I really want to be fair
I really want to
Respect
Appreciate
Understand
The other women
That my husband fucks

But I just can't seem to do it

One of them is suburban
I am urban
Another one is a cog in the wheel of a giant company
I am a kickass-and-take-names business owner
And yet another only left the mainland for her honeymoon
I have travelled the world for business and pleasure
We have NOTHING in common
EXCEPT for my husbands cock

I'm sure they are nice
Take care of their husbands and kids

Attend PTA meetings
And concern themselves about simple things each day like me

But
They crave my husbands cock
And that just doesn't sit well with me

I started off calling one his Metamour
But I realized he didn't love her
And since she doesn't want him involved in her life
(outside of a hotel room)
The other couldn't be his OSO either
So, I finally started calling them all his FWB
But they don't do anything that friends would do
(i.e. play games, see a movie, etc.)
So they doesn't fit that description either
He only sees them to meet in a hotel room
After a text earlier in the day
So, I have finally labeled them all Booty Call.

I guess it doesn't much matter
What label they get
They have disrupted my peaceful world

18th – How to destroy passion: Or why polyamory sucks.

There is plenty to read these days about how great polyamory is great for improving your sex life at home. Hell, even CNN and Cosmo have gotten in on the act. It's mainstream or a fad depending on your POV.

Some even say that being poly will improve your sex life.
Recent studies show that secondaries apparently get more sex than primaries
I wonder how the other primaries in the world feel about that
I know I don't like that since I've had a very high libido all my adult life

My personal experience: it destroyed my libido and the sex with my husband

Much science says that sexual passion will fade over time.
That it is inevitable.
That was NOT my experience.

My husband have been together over a decade
Our sex life was rich, full and very active
We explored
We tried new things
We had sex a lot (yay!)
I was able to fully open myself to him
And let him reach the places inside that no man ever had before

Then he poly-bombed me.

It has successfully crushed me
Broken my spirit
Leaving me empty
And so alone
And without desire or passion
Of any kind
At least someone is having a good time
Even if it isn't me

23rd – Tick Tock

Tick Tock

Tick Tock

Tick Tock

Time is ticking by
How much do we have?
I think to myself

Tick Tock

Everything about our life is
Perfect
Blissful
Wonderful
Romantic
EXCEPT
That you say you need to fuck other women

Tick Tock

I know
I've said it all before and before
And it is still true

I adore you
I belong to you
We snuggle
Bill and coo

You tease
I blush
Our desire grows
And then
Just when it seems like
The time

Tick tock

To be intimate
To share ourselves
In the most special way possible
To revel in the elusive love
That so many fail to find
I freeze

Tick Tock

My head swims
My body tenses
My breathe is ragged
My stomach lurches
Tears flow from my eyes

Tick Tock

You stop
And hold me tightly
Reassuring me
Of your love and desire
While I sob inconsolably
Mourning what we have lost

Tick Tock

I hope you can feel
My heart breaking
My soul in anguish
As I struggle
To open myself
And realize the precious gift
We share together
While my heart shuts down

Tick Tock

How long can this last?
How long will you continue to express your love?
How long until you decide I'm not worth waiting for?

Tick Tock

I hear the clock
And the time ticking away
Slipping away
I hope your love and desire for me
Is not going with it

30th – Leaks

You say you are afraid of me
You say you can't trust me
You say you can't trust what I say
To be true

When I say, "it's ok"
I want it to be true
When I say, "please go do whatever you want"
I want it to be true
When I say, "it doesn't hurt me"
I want it to be true

You say that I stuff the hurt
Until it leaks out
In the form of tears
Or, worse
In other ways
In ugly ways
Upon other people
In the form of anger
And rage

That is true
Despite my not wanting it to be so
I don't know what to do
To care for myself
I keep trying to find the solution
The way to keep myself from hurting
Besides stuffing and ignoring

I'm trying to journal
My gratitude
For all that I have
To let me feel the wonder
And incredible passion
Of my life
That's not making a difference
Yet
Because the hurt and anger
Are still leaking out

I'm drinking too much
And that doesn't help
That just removes my filters
And the leakage comes quicker
And in less-appropriate ways
The anti-anxiety/depression meds
Aren't doing it either
I tempted to try something stronger
Maybe valium
Something to numb me

I know I need to address
Whatever deep hurt
Is festering within me
But I haven't been able
To find it and give it
The love so it can go on it's way
I really want the pain to leak out
And never come back

CHAPTER 10
The Glimmer of Hope

JULY

Recognizing my angst and anguish, I express my desire for a joyful life again. I know I can have it, even though I'm not sure how to get to that place.

I no longer trust anyone. Including my daughter since she is now a part of his lies (I sensed this although I only discovered this after we separate). I only trust myself and my abilities. I am alone and cannot seek assistance from anyone.

I've decided that I'll fake it until I make it.

Here comes a turning point, a moment where amidst the darkness, a glimmer of hope emerges. You'll see me acknowledging the depth of my pain, but also expressing a fundamental belief that joy is still possible.

This is a chapter about the first steps towards reclaiming one's life, even when the path is unclear.

As you read, you'll see me making a decision to put on a brave face and keep moving forward, even when every ounce of my soul wants to give up.

It's a reminder that even in our darkest hours, there is a part of us that yearns for joy, that believes in the possibility of a better future.

18th – Success

I am successful

Successful at:

- shutting down
- shutting you out
- hurting you
- hurting the people around me
- isolating myself
- sinking deeper into depression
- letting my deep hurt become rage
- letting the rage consume me
- shutting down your love for me
- filling my house with tears and angst
- making my home a place to escape from

It's time to be more successful

Successful at:

- finding the good in all things
- allowing these lessons to move through me
- change my experience
- change the reality for the people around me
- get over my fears and pains
- trusting myself
- rebuilding your trust
- doing the things that create love

- love myself
- be grateful
- learn my lessons (finally)
- make space for your love

In short, I will rock my life

Again.

26th – Judgement

Everything I've known is gone
The only thing I have is me
I am alone

I must trust the universe
To find balance
I want balance

Right now, I want to hide myself
I can't trust others
My husband
My daughter
My friends
My parents

I am the only one
To trust
With all of me
I will
Listen to the universe
And find my path
To walk alone

I need to hide
Silence the things that others judge
I fear all the ugly
I fear the frightened parts of me
Because they are judged by others
They are not welcomed by others

I cannot trust anyone
I cannot trust my husband
He judges me

I miss being myself
But only I can see the true me
Only I can accept the true me

28th – Happy

I am happy

Ok, so not 100% happy
But I've decided
That I will be

They say, 'fake it until you make it'

I am happy
For the most part
And I will be
Within myself

I will no longer
Let others impact
My happy
It is mine

I will do the things that make me happy
Some of those include others
Some don't
Having both is the only way to be
Happy
And healthy
- Self-care = happy
- 'Me time' = happy
- Love = happy
- Caring for my family = happy

- Reading = happy
- Friends = happy
- Work = happy
- Road biking = extra starburst happy
- Smiling = happy
- Music = happy
- Coffee = happy

All of those things and so many more are what make me happy

I am owning happy
I don't need things to be perfect to be happy
(Although, I think some of my desire to be perfect has made me and others unhappy in the past.)
Happiness surrounds me and fills me
I share my happy
Because I have it in abundance
It oozes from me
And surrounds me
Embraces me

Happy = Me

CHAPTER 11
The Struggle of Acceptance

AUGUST

I'm still believing my husband's story about being poly, even though I know it is a lie. Friends, acquaintances, and those in the poly/mono groups I'm in who have met him say that he is a selfish narcissist. I don't really know, since it is beyond my comprehension that any human being could be completely without empathy.

A part of me has decided that I will not depend upon him for love or caring anymore. I can't if I want to survive. I have to care for myself. Care enough to do things that will help me.

I'm still crying. A lot.

I struggle coming to terms with my painful reality. You'll see me grappling with the dissonance between what my husband tells me and what I feel along with what everyone around me is saying.

I'll take you through the process of trying to comprehend the incomprehensible - the idea that someone could be entirely devoid of empathy. You'll feel the resistance, the part of me that doesn't want to believe it could be true.

This is a chapter about the beginning of a big shift, a realization that I can no longer rely on my husband for the love and care I need. It's a testament to the strength it takes to start prioritizing one's own well-being. My survival depends on my ability to detach from the hope of receiving what I need from my husband.

This chapter is a reminder that progress isn't linear, that even as we start to understand what we need to do, we still feel the pain of the situation acutely.

It's a chapter that many who have been in similar situations will find deeply relatable. The struggle to accept a reality we don't want to be true, the grief that comes with letting go of the hope that the person we love will change.

2nd – Selfishness vs. Selflessness

Selfishness
Concerned excessively or exclusively with oneself: seeking or concentrating on one's own advantage, pleasure or well-being without regard for others

Selflessness
Having no concern for self

Extremes
In opposite directions
There is, and should be, a whole mess of grey in the middle

It is argued by some that practicing polyamory is selfish.
Far more (at least those in the poly world) like to say that monogamy is selfish.
Go ahead. Google it and see what you get
The poly community does a fabulous job
Of making their case
Of being more:
- Enlightened
- Accepting
- Open-Minded

I keep having friends
Tell me
That my husband is selfish
Not because he identifies as poly
But because of his actions towards me

Three of these friends self-identify as poly
(Just in case you think they don't accept poly as a lifestyle)

One has told him to his face
That his behavior is selfish
And destructive
She referred to gaslighting
As his way of controlling me
And getting his way

One was more diplomatic
Calling him self-absorbed

Another keeps telling me that
By him not wanting
To admit that he doesn't want to
Make our marriage work
Would make him the bad guy
And damage his ego
He would rather me
Leave
So he can say I was the one
That wouldn't make our marriage
Work
Freeing him to keep his ego intact
She says poly
WITHOUT
True consent
(Meaning that all parties are happily onboard)
Is abuse

Does that mean I'm abused?
I don't know

I don't think so
I guess I'm confused
And trying so hard to accept
What he tells me he needs
Connection
With other women
Telling me it isn't about the sex
Doesn't feel truthful
When you expect to have it

Am I displaying selflessness?
Am I concerned for myself?
Absolutely
Am I concerned for my marriage?
Hell yes!
Do I need my husband and marriage?
Hell no!
I'm very capable of taking care of myself
I'm not here because I'm afraid
Of being alone
I'm here because
This relationship
Is very special and valuable to me
I don't have to be with him all the time
Or even want to
But I do like sharing life with him
For now

I'm reading Co-dependant No More
Again
It's been 20 years
I originally read it

When I was leaving
An alcoholic
Do I enable?
To my own detriment?
Maybe
Maybe not
But self-care is my mantra
And only I can heal me

7th – Moving Day

I'm feeling lighter lately.
Closer to myself (pre-polybomb*)
The question I have is why?

Am I finally accepting my husband's desire for other women?
Have I faced my demons about:
- abandonment
- infidelity (previous relationships)
- being undesirable
- unworthiness

Am I just too tired of being hurt after all these years?
Am I too fatigued to be angry about the loss?
Am I done grieving for the loss of the bliss with my husband?
Am I becoming hard-hearted?
Am I too tired to care anymore?

I worry that I don't care enough anymore
Worry is too strong a word
More like, sad
Sad
Sad that I'm becoming apathetic
Sad
Sad that I'm moving on
Without him
And him with me

Sad
Sad that I won't care
Or trust

Anyone
Ever
Keeping myself
Aloof
Distant
Protecting the parts that only he ever touched

I had the perfect
Bliss
Cherished
And wonderful
The thing that all humans seek
Connection
With another
Baring
Your heart and soul
Baring
Your ugly bits
And still feeling loved
Baring
Your soft, squishy parts
Knowing that you are safe
Safe
In his arms
Safe
In his heart

Gone now
Blasted to bits
Disrupted
By his need
By his uncompromising selfishness

Pouring my heart to him
Day after day
Night after night
Attempting to accept him
And his detachment
His willingness to
Throw away
The bliss
We had
Wholly

I guess it's moving day
Moving on
Emotionally
Without him
Because he no longer
Likes me
Wants me
Desires me

*I find it interesting that the term poly-bombed is used so frequently (usually by the partner that was bombed) but if you try to Google the term; crickets. The poly community seems to ignore the incredibly explosive and destructive impact that 'the bomb' has on their partner. I suggest y'all own the term. Own the hurt and damage you do to the ones you so-call love. This isn't all fun and games. We are taking about real people with very real feelings.

12th – Salty

I keep saying that
I'm done
Crying
Sobbing
Mourning
The grief
Of losing
Something
So special

And yet
I still cry
Sometimes uncontrollably
Letting the salty tears
Roll down my face
Soaking my shirt
And pillow

It's tiring
And zaps my strength
Especially
Since I have to hide it
Any emotion
That isn't positive
Is shunned
Judged
By all those around me

21st – Parallel Lines

Parallels
Between polyamory and monogamy

Monogamy has many friendships
Platonic
Emotionally fulfilling

Polyamory has many friendships
Sexual
Sometimes emotionally fulfilling*

You say
Your poly relationships
Enrich you
Thereby
Enriching
Our relationship

Mentally
I accept
This position
You hold

Emotionally
I crumble
My friendships
Don't threaten our relationship

You say
You don't want limits
On anything
On your friendships

I accept you
Unconditionally

But we know
It isn't working
The way we are doing it
Right now
Something
Anything
Needs to change

I feel
Lost inside
Adorable illusion
And I cannot hide
I'm the one you're using
Please don't push me aside
We coulda made it cruising

---

* *Some will take exception to my statement that sometimes polyamorous relationships are emotionally fulfilling. I'm sure there are monogamous relationships that are not emotionally fulfilling and some polyamorous relationships that are. I only speak from my own personal experience.*

CHAPTER 12
The Non-Linear Path of Healing

SEPTEMBER

I'm working through (or trying to) the stages of grief. Here I'm hoping I'm in the Acceptance stage, but since healing isn't linear, I know I move between them all.

I'm still trying to hang onto the original illusion of our marriage.

My husband is intensely gaslighting me about his mistress. He has only one now (I think). He became infatuated with the woman working for him, even though he and she would be fired for the transgression. (Despite me asking him about her, his lies become more flimsy. He even brought our 14-year-old daughter into the secret. Sick.)

You can see the complex, non-linear nature of the healing process. You'll see me navigating the stages of grief, hoping to have reached acceptance, but realizing that I move back and forth between the stages.

You'll feel the part of me that still wants to cling to the illusion of our perfect marriage, even in the face of overwhelming evidence to the contrary.

This is a chapter about the insidious nature of gaslighting, about how it can make you question your own reality. This takes a tremendous toll on me and the way it makes me question my own perceptions.

There are complex emotions that come with this stage of the journey. The hope of having reached acceptance, the pain of seeing the truth of the situation in stark relief.

As you witness this part of the journey, you may find validation for your own experiences of the non-linear path of healing. May it serve as a reminder that moving back and forth between stages is normal, and that clinging to illusions is a part of the process of letting go.

3rd – Stages

According to some theories, there are 5 stages of grief.

1. Denial
2. Anger
3. Bargaining
4. Depression
5. Acceptance

I've been grieving on and off for years since my husband poly-bombed me. The grief has been hyper-focused on the past year. To be fair, he has always been transparent about his desires and actions. He has never lied to me about his behavior or whereabouts.

Denial = Shock

I was shaken to my core when my husband told me that he identified as polyamorous. I didn't understand it.

- Weren't we happy?
- What was lacking in me?
- Why did he marry me if he wanted other women?
- Didn't we have a rich (and kinky) sex life?

Yes, according to him but he felt limited. He wanted to experience life without limits, including having intimate relationships with other women.

Because of my past experiences (being cheated on several times), he chose NOT to act upon this revelation. I felt betrayed; this wasn't what I signed up for.

Pain = Reality

When he said he needed to act upon his desires. I felt overwhelmed and started by self-medicated with alcohol and cigarettes* while he went out and found sex with other women. The pain was so powerful that I became incredibly anxious; prone to crying at the least little thing. The pain was debilitating and I found it difficult to get out of bed in the mornings. I couldn't focus on anything.

The pain hasn't left me but I have learned to function.

Anger = Rage

My pain reached the level of destruction. I was self-destructing. On the inside for the most part although I found myself losing my temper and taking it out on people that didn't deserve my rage directed at them.
Occasionally, I raged at my husband for his choices. I wouldn't let him touch me and I was icy cold at times. I shut down my feelings and let him have my body but I was damned if I would let him touch my soul again. He didn't deserve me. I was untouchable to him. To anyone really.

I'm not proud of lashing out at others or my husband since it didn't help anyone.

Depression = Hiding

Most of this year, I've been depressed. Hiding myself. I stopped seeing my friends and doing things that previously brought me joy. I just couldn't be around people when all I wanted to do was sob. Sleep was a welcome escape and I did a lot of it. I wanted my cancer from 3 years ago to return and take me away from this life of pain and hurt.

Nothing brought me joy. My friends knew something was wrong but I removed myself from being around them through my previous regular activities. My friends couldn't help. How could I tell him that my husband wanted to fuck other women without them judging him or me? They wouldn't understand or probably even try. Medications didn't help even though I took them.

I couldn't stop sinking lower and lower. I was lost in the darkness while I reached for it. I still got up each day and attempted to care for myself but it became increasingly harder. The only thing helping was that I needed to care for and love my daughter and run my business (which amazingly, has doubled in size during the past year). I went to therapy and was diagnosed as clinically depressed.

Acceptance = Am I there yet?

My depression has lifted slightly. I no longer drink or smoke to numb myself. I don't breakdown hourly into uncontrollable tears. I don't know that I understand what changed except I'm just focusing on me. I list the things I'm grateful for each day, even though it is a stretch some days. I read, cycle, plan and take trips by myself and have slowly started to see my friends again.

At the end of the day, the truth of the matter is that my life will never the same.

My husband seems to be the one that is lost now. I only work on me and have left him to find himself. If he has to do it in the arms of other women, then so be it.

The stages aren't necessarily in a linear order but occur at different times. I know, I've had them all at the same time I think.

I have chosen to love and accept him and his choices unconditionally. I am moving forward and have good days and not-so-good days as I continue to navigate my way through the stages.

I don't smoke and never have in my life. I wanted to hurt myself.

24th – Scar*ci*ty

scar•ci•ty
'skersede/
Noun
The state of being scarce or in short supply; shortage

That is what it is
I don't like
About this poly thing

When I think about all things
I have to do each day
- be an enterpreur
- parent a teenager
- manage the household
- care for the female menagerie at our house
    - 1 cat, 1 dog, 3 backyard chickens
- have 'me' time

Along with the
Things you do
- be a SVP with a team of 60
- travel 60% of the time
- parent a teenager
- have 'me' time

Leaves little time for
US
To enjoy each other
We used to do that
With every little moment
We were together

Even if it was just the time
We get to snuggle at night

BUT
When you aren't home for days
And then go to one of them
It leaves me
Beyond sad
More like
Forgotten
Unlovable
Unwanted

And now
You take your
Affection away
Because you feel trapped
With me

The scarcity of time together
Is what I don't like
One
Little
Bit

CHAPTER 13
The Unraveling

OCTOBER

The life I created, we created, is actively falling apart at the seams. Because my husband had to have it his way. His way was going around and fucking anything in a skirt that he wanted.

Now our daughter, a teen with enough to deal with, was made complicit in your affair. She found a way to deal with the turmoil at home by getting drugs and generally being unsafe. You told me to leave her alone. Not to worry about her since she was a teen and going to be a bit messy. I worried and you berated me.

The devastating consequences of my husband's narcissistic behavior have not only destroyed our marriage but also deeply affected our daughter.

I'll take you through the heartbreak of watching the life we built together unravel, all because of my husband's selfish desires. You'll feel the anger and betrayal of knowing he prioritized his own wants over the well-being of our family.

This is a chapter about the far-reaching impact of narcissistic abuse, about how it can shatter not just the relationship between partners, but the entire family system. You'll witness the pain of seeing our daughter drawn into the toxic dynamics, and her struggle to cope with the turmoil.

There are additional burdens placed on me as a mother. The worry for my daughter's safety, the instinct to protect her, and the crushing weight of my husband's dismissal and criticism of my concerns.

This chapter is a portrayal of the chaos and trauma that narcissistic abuse can inflict on a family. It's a reminder that the consequences are not confined to the relationship between the narcissist and their partner, but ripple out to affect everyone connected to them.

It's a chapter that may resonate deeply with anyone who has watched their family unravel due to a narcissist's actions. The pain of seeing your children suffer, the frustration of having your concerns dismissed, the anger at the narcissist's selfishness.

14th – Is Poly Hell?

I guess it depends on who you talk to
And how you get to poly

If, as Kathy Labriola states in her 'Are you in poly hell?' post,
You stumble upon it
By choice
Or chance
If you are monogamous
(Or mostly monogamous)
You will probably suffer
In the following ways:

Demotion
When going from being the center of my Master's universe
To one of two (or more)
Was more than a little distressing
The changes
Are scary
Saying he doesn't love me any less
While giving some of his time and affection
To someone else
Is so very painful

Open communication
Happens
As does negotiation
My attempts
To be adult

And establish clear boundaries
And express my needs

All while experiencing
Sadness
Betrayal
Grief
Abandonment
Saying that it isn't so
Causes me to feel invalidated
And no longer
Important

Displacement
To be fair
My Master never went
To one of them
So much that our relationship
Was winnowed out completely (although, it's very close)

I felt
Isolated
Unloveable
Broken
Nonetheless

Work
Travel
Life
Kids
Happen

Leaving 'us' time
Limited
So any time taken from
The little bit we have
Leaves me feeling replaced
By someone more interesting

Intrusion
I understand
That you want to
Give time
And attention
To this new person
To make this relationship
Work
And thrive

These women invade our happy home
When you come home
Smelling of one of them
When your phone
Pings
Or
You are hiding
Emails
Communications
Or sharing one of their homes
With 'her'
Or your ex
(Or any other woman
That wants you)
Openly flirts
With you

It drives a stake
Through my heart
Over
And over
And over
Until there is no more
Blood to bleed

All I want
Is protection
Of our relationship
The special
Thing
That makes us
Full of bliss
Protect me from poly hell

16th – It's All Gone

Or, how to destroy your live and the lives of those you love in a short time through polyamory.

So you say you want freedom?
You say love is unlimited
And should not be contained
You need to love intimately
With whom ever you want
Regardless of promises and commitments previously made
You say you love everyone equally
For all are uniquely special
But how can that be true?

People change
You have changed
Circumstances change
And you changed them
Disregarding the impact on others
And how others may be hurt
By your actions
NRE happens
Life happens

It happened to us
When you decided that you HAD
To have it your way
To explore yourself
Explore your freedom
Explore other women

Explore anything that excluded me
And how anyone else felt was inconsequential
Especially me

I wanted to give you the freedom
But I guess I'm not as 'enlightened' as you
Not cool enough to be around your friends
Too larger than life for you to be yourself
It hurt me
Hurt me deeply

Pushed me to the brink
I wanted to die
I wanted the hurt to end
I couldn't trust you anymore
Not to hurt me

I shut down
I couldn't kiss you
Without thinking you wished you were with one of them
Those that had no thought or concern
Of what was our simple, blissful lives
It wasn't them anyway
They were just a symptom
Of your selfishness

I loved you anyway
I still do
Did everything for you and our daughter
But you said you felt trapped
By the responsibilities
You created for yourself

You decided
To pay me back in spades
You needed to be sad
To repay my sadness
By being sad enough to
Reject me totally
Reject any love from me
Reject me wholly
And starve me of your love
Leaving me more desolate than ever

Then our precious child
Drifted away
To negative influences
To escape the tension at home
She found solace in the drugs and sex
Provided so willingly by a kid without
Parents loving enough to care about him

And so, here we are
She is expelled
And in treatment
For drugs and anger
You are hopeless
And I feel like I can only show love and compassion
To hold onto the precious family
That is so very special to me

You managed to obliterate everything
With your selfishness
You will never see it

Because of your ability to only
See the universe revolve around you
But you did this
You and your demand for the
Perfect illusion of polyamory
Destroyed the happiness
And lives of yourself and everyone around you
It's almost gone now

CHAPTER 14
The Breaking Point and the Beginning of Healing

NOVEMBER

I recognize that adversity is an opportunity. An opportunity to find something new. Something better.

My husband is still trying to convince me that he is not doing anything wrong but asked me to move out of the house for the sake of our daughter. Because, in his words, I'm the one needing mental health care and she should not be around me. I sob and ask where would I go. I do nothing.

Then, one day, he announces he is moving out of the house (he couldn't get me out so he is leaving). This was my breaking point. I ended up in the hospital for a week after a failed suicide attempt. They didn't want to send me home after meeting him.

While I was in the hospital, he had a date every day with the current mistress (and my daughter was with them). He removed his wedding ring.

This was the beginning of me actually accepting that he had been abusing me. The start of a long healing process that led me back to joy.

This was the darkest moment of my journey, but also the first glimmers of hope and healing. You'll see me grappling with the realization that my husband's actions are abusive, and the devastating impact this had on my mental health.

His continued gaslighting, his attempts to manipulate me into leaving our home, and the shattering moment when he decides to leave himself. You'll feel the despair that drove me to attempt to end my life.

This is a chapter about hitting rock bottom, about the moment when the full weight of the narcissistic abuse becomes undeniable. It's a portrayal of the depth of pain that can be inflicted by a narcissist's actions, and the life-threatening consequences of their manipulation.

The hospital's recognition of the abuse, the refusal to send me back into a toxic environment, marks a turning point. It's the beginning of my journey towards accepting the reality of my situation and starting to heal.

This chapter is a testament to the resilience of the human spirit, to the possibility of finding hope and healing even in the darkest of moments. It's a reminder that hitting rock bottom can be the catalyst for change, the start of a journey towards reclaiming one's life and joy.

You may find echoes of your own experiences. May it serve as a reminder that you are not alone, that healing is possible, and that even the darkest moments can lead to a brighter future.

3rd – The Obstacle Is The Path

The obstacle is the way
I feel this
Deeply
I embrace this
Opportunity
To enrich my life
And yours

Where are we?

In love
Still (I think)
But working
To define
Our relationship
Ourselves
Our family

Why?
Why do I stay?
Why do you stay?

I can't speak for you
But
I can dig
Deep inside myself
And understand
Why I'm still here

I haven't given up
On you
On our daughter
On our relationship
On myself

I made a commitment
To you
To our daughter
To myself
For good or bad

I gave my heart
Willing
Because I had faith
In the strength of our love
I still do

Just because it gets hard
Harder
Than I've ever experienced
Doesn't mean I ditch
Escape the pain

That would be too easy
A copout
I'm not one to do that
The softness within me
Still exists
Yes, it hurts
But it makes the ultimate bliss
That much sweeter

I am the only obstacle
In my path
To happiness

22nd – Adrift

Yesterday
My husband
Told me
He is done
With me

Done
Trying to be happy
Done
Trying to find the path
With me

Giving up
Coping out
Not keeping his word
For better or worse

Yes
Now it is worse
It's time to throw it all away

That means
It's time to evolve
And grow

I'm ready

EPILOGUE
A Survivor's Reflection

13 MONTHS LATER
DECEMBER

In this final chapter, I reflect on my journey, the lessons I've learned, and the hope I've found. It's about the possibility of survival and healing even after the darkest of experiences.

As you read, you'll see me coming to terms with the reality of my husband's abuse, recognizing the signs that were there all along. You'll witness the pain of realizing that his love was never real, that I was simply another source of supply for his own emptiness.

I'll share the hard-earned wisdom of my journey to recovery. The necessity of taking responsibility for one's own healing, of recognizing and owning the ways in which we tolerated the intolerable. It's a message of empowerment, of the importance of self-love and self-care in the healing process.

You'll see that recovery is not a straightforward path, that there will be setbacks and challenges along the way. But you'll also see the hope that emerges, the gradual return of joy and the realization that life can be beautiful again.

This epilogue is a message of hope, a reminder that survival and healing are possible. It's a call to anyone who has experienced narcissistic abuse to keep going, to believe in themselves and their right to a life free from abuse.

As you close this book, may you take with you the strength and resilience of a survivor. May you know that you are not alone, that healing is possible, and that a life of joy and freedom awaits you.

12th – I'm Alive

I'm still alive.
After surviving 11 years of narcissistic abuse
That's saying something
I almost didn't survive
As I read the two years of blog posts for the first time since I was willing to actually listen and hear our marriage therapist of 6 years along with the warnings of good friends, I realize how he truly never cared for me, himself or anyone else for that matter
I shudder to read what was so clearly the signs of abuse by my husband
I cringe as I read my sanity slipping further away from his subtle gaslighting

The blog clearly shows the distress
Felt during the final brutal discard phase of this invisible abuse

And even after I attempted to take my own life,
As I witnessed the mask make the final slip to display the cruel apathy of his true colors
I still questioned my own sanity
That is how well he had ingrained the trauma bonding

I am a cautionary tale.
A tale of a smart, beautiful woman
Taken in by a covert narcissist
Looking for prime supply to avoid his own inner turmoil and insecurities

Recovery from narcissistic abuse is a journey is not for the faint of heart

You will need to own your piece of the experience
This is not victim-shaming
This is willing to love yourself enough
To recognize that
You tolerated the intolerable

Nor is the recovery process linear
You will make great progress
Only to tumble on a single step and fall to the floor (or two) below

I can only share that when you slip,
Get back up
Do the things to care for yourself each day
Eat right, limit alcohol, exercise, meditate
Even when you don't feel like doing them
These self-care behaviors are essential to your recovery

Eventually, you will see a glimmer of hope
A light sneaking under the door
To show you that living is still lovely and wonderful

RESOURCES TO THRIVE AFTER NARCISSISTIC ABUSE

Books

Arabi, Shahida. (2016). Becoming the Narcissist's Nightmare: How to Devalue and Discard the Narcissist While Supplying Yourself. SCW Archer Publishing.

Davenport, Barrie. (2016). Signs of Emotional Abuse: How to Recognize the Patterns of Narcissism, Manipulation, and Control in Your Love Relationship. CreateSpace.

Mirza, Debbie. (2017). The Covert Passive Aggressive Narcissist: Recognizing the Traits and Finding Healing After Hidden Emotional and Psychological Abuse. Debbie Mirza Coaching.

Northrup, Christiane. (2018). Dodging Energy Vampires: An Empath's Guide to Evading Relationships That Drain You and Restoring Your Health and Power. Hay House.

Resnick, Meredith. (2014). Surviving the Narcissist: 30 Days of Recovery: Whether You're Loving, Leaving or Living With One. BookBaby.

Meditations
Insight Timer
I was fortunate to find Insight Timer shortly after the beginning of the end had started. I had struggled to meditate for years until I discovered the guided meditations here. Insight Timer is the best meditation app with the world's largest FREE library of more than 200k guided meditations, 17k teachers & the world's most loved meditation app.

Since I was deep in the process of recovering from narcissistic abuse, I was looking for meditations that would guide me. Here is a list of some of the favorites that have helped me.

Awaken to a Clean Slate
Becoming
Body Scan Exploration
Cultivating a Healthy Boundary
Detach and Release Toxic Ties
From Pain to Peace
Releasing Fear and Doubt Caused by Others
The Power of No Contact
You Deserve

Healing Programs
Lisa Romano
To be completely honest, I haven't taken any of Lisa's workshops but have listened to her talks on Insight Timer.

LNAL Life
Overcoming Narcissistic Abuse Challenge
This is a 10-day challenge to provide knowledge and practical tools to begin the journey of healing from narcissistic abuse.

Melanie Tonia Evans
This expert on narcissistic abuse recovery, healer, author, and radio host provides healing methods that allow you to thrive. Her Narcissistic Abuse Recovery Program (NARP) walks you through the healing process to create an abuse-free life. I went through the NARP program and regularly revisit it.

www.ingramcontent.com/pod-product-compliance
Lightning Source LLC
Chambersburg PA
CBHW032112090426
42743CB00007B/322